Table of Contents

Objectives	3
Doulas Instill Strength and Reduce Fear	5
Non-Judgmental Support	6
Attunement	6
Determining Personality: DISC	8
Contributing Factors to Negativity Around Birth	12
Birth Trauma	12
Obstetrical Violence/Systemic Bias/Medical Racism	13
Maternal and Infant Mortality Rates	14
Birth Philosophies	16
Understanding the Birth Environment	19
Universal Precautions for Birth Workers	19
Birth Settings	20
Friedman's Curve	25
Patient's Bill of Rights	26
Birth - It's a Hormonal Process	27
Supporting Labor	29
Cervical Changes During Chilbirth	32
Stages of Labor	34
Rituals Associated with Labor	36
Assertive/Accommodating Approach	37
Second Stage - Pushing	39
Third Stage - The Placenta	40
Delayed Umbilical Cord Clamping	41
Laboring at Home: When You Will, When You Won't	42
Induction of Labor	43
Bishop Score	43
Interventions & Medications	45
Rupture of Membranes	47
Braxton-Hicks Contractions	49
Timing Contractions	49
Sharing the Benefits of Doula Support	53
Elevator Speech	53
Doula Consultations	55
Prenatal Schedule for Healthy Pregnancies	56
Writing a Birth Plan	59
Spontaneous Labor	60
Prodromal Labor	61
Precipitous Labor	61
Code Word	63

Support When Plans Change	66
Placenta Encapsulation	68
Getting Comfortable with Touch	69
Comfort Measures	71
Partner Support	73
Labor Positions	74
Pushing Positions	75
Further Interventions/Medications	81
Episiotomy	85
Epidurals	87
Cesarean Birth	92
VBAC Guidelines	97
Breech	100
Challenging Childbirth	102
Immediate Postpartum and the Newborn	104
The Basics of Early Bodyfeeding	107
Postpartum Follow-Up Visit	111
Doula Self Care	113
Life of a Doula	113
Entry Level Business for Doulas	116
Labor Doula Support Contract	123
Business Forms	127
Marketing Your Doula Business	128
Streams of Income for Your Doula Business	130
Growing Your Doula Business	130
Goal Setting	131

Objectives

Congratulations on taking the first step toward becoming a professional labor doula! We are honored that you have chosen ProDoula as your training and certification organization and we look forward to supporting you every step of the way.

This comprehensive labor doula training will provide you with the necessary skills to support future clients during pregnancy, labor, and birth. Through this standardized curriculum and the inspired dialogue that accompanies it in your training, you will deepen your understanding of birth philosophies, birth environments, the stages of labor, medical and non-medical interventions, and so much more. You will learn how to physically and emotionally support clients from the very first prenatal consultation, through the uncertainties surrounding the onset of labor, and all the way through to the immediate postpartum period.

One of ProDoula's founding principles is professional, non-judgmental support. Therefore, this training will equip you with the skills to support clients seeking unmedicated births, medicated births, and cesarean births. As a ProDoula doula, the bias or preferences you have toward or against various ideas or procedures surrounding birth must remain your own so that you can provide your clients with the non-judgmental support they desire.

This labor doula training provides the space and time for processing personal thoughts and experiences regarding birth. It is essential that each learner work through any difficult birth scenarios they may have experienced in order to avoid impacting clients' births in a negative way.

During this course, you will learn about DISC, a personality assessment tool that pertains to improved communication. By better understanding how different people communicate and process information, you will learn to attune to any client you serve and provide them with the best possible support suited to their individual personality. Your knowledge of DISC will also assist you in attracting and securing clients. You may even enhance some existing personal relationships with this newly learned skill.

You will be given step-by-step instructions on how to complete your certification following this training. ProDoula values certification and encourages you to complete this process.

The accompanying comprehensive certification exam is part of your training. The research you will do to complete the exam will broaden and build on your skills and knowledge.

And finally, this labor doula training will introduce you to the specifics of establishing a professional doula business. ProDoula is committed to elevating the role of the doula to a professional level and encourages each individual to enjoy a long and fulfilling career in this rewarding field.

Following this labor doula training, the doula will be able to:

- Provide emotional, educational, and physical support to clients seeking labor doula support
- Demonstrate a comprehensive understanding of the stages of labor, the various induction methods, varying philosophies regarding birth choices, and will have the ability to provide exceptional support in each scenario
- Understand and evaluate each client's personality style and attune to them in order to better support each individual client and their partner
- Know the steps needed to establish a legitimate doula business and understand the key tenets of how to run a successful business that attracts clients
- Follow the steps needed to become a ProDoula Certified Labor Doula

Doulas Instill Strength and Reduce Fear, However...

There are a few things that a doula is not. A doula is not a medical professional and does not provide clinical/medical care, such as examinations, assessments, or monitoring. The doula does not make medical or philosophical decisions for the client or speak on their behalf. The doula can help them interpret scenarios, provide information for decision-making, and prepare the client with the proper language to best communicate their choices. The doula works for the client and simultaneously maintains a cohesive relationship with the client's caregivers.

The doula is not an advocate. Advocacy is any action that speaks in favor of, recommends, argues for a cause, supports or defends, or pleads on behalf of others.

The doula's role in advocacy is to provide support.

When a doula uses their voice to advocate for a client's desires, rather than encouraging the client to advocate for themselves, the doula becomes empowered. Supporting a client by offering them the encouragement and the language to advocate for themselves, empowers the client. A doula does this by reminding the client of their wishes or birth preferences and creating space and opportunity for the client to use their own voice.

Advocating for oneself is a skill that is learned through experience. Having the support of a doula during labor can assist in establishing strong communication between the client and their providers, enabling the birthing person to confidently advocate for their wishes. No communication can be facilitated or self-empowerment achieved when the doula speaks on behalf of the client.

Legally, the client, not the doula, must either consent or decline to any procedure or intervention during labor.

Doulas help create change when they are respected and invited to contribute to conversations where obstetrical policies are made. By becoming a respected colleague, you can advocate (outside of the birth room) for the necessary systemic change that benefits all birthing individuals.

The ProDoula philosophy is based on the desire to elevate the role of doulas to a professional level in the eyes of expectant individuals and partners, medical professionals, and doulas themselves.

The word doula represents a profession, not a philosophy. Unfortunately, some doulas have created a stereotype for themselves (and you) that can mislead potential clients to think that you will look and behave a certain way. A potential client that is more "mainstream" may be anxious about hiring a doula because of those stereotypes. You can help change these concerns by being the most professional, accountable, and respectful version of yourself.

Non-Judgmental Support

A judgmental person is someone who categorizes people based on observations. Judgment comes in the form of actions and facial expressions, not just verbal communication. By pure definition, there can be a positive and a negative side to passing judgment. For example, a client may not categorize their parenting style because they are not familiar with the terms. By observing the way they care for their baby or keep to schedules you, the doula, can judge that they lean more towards attachment parenting than scheduled parenting or vice versa.

By using non-judgmental support we can make observations that lead to decisions about how to best support the client. When working with a new family, it is important to remember that they may be feeling insecure about their expectations or ideas regarding parenting. They are being judged by family members and friends regarding every detail they share. From baby names to breast pumps, everyone has an opinion...except you, their doula.

You are there to provide support. Your support comes in a judgment-free package. You give options and resources that enable people to make the best choices for themselves and you encourage them to embrace those choices. Your job is to enable each client to feel confident about the choices they make for themselves and their families.

Attunement

"To bring into a harmonious or responsive relationship"

This is the definition of attunement and it is an essential ingredient in the doula/client interaction.

The client must know that their doula will understand them and that their doula "speaks their language." This is one of the ways that trust and comfort is established.

The client does not know how they will behave during labor. Feeling a sense of attunement with their doula can bring them the freedom to "let go" during the experience. With a sense of attunement comes feelings of safety and security. Attunement is the very concept that doula support is built on.

As a doula, you must have the ability to connect with your clients. Sometimes that means letting go of your own style of communication and adapting to theirs. Being aware of how the client best receives ideas and information enables you to give it to them in the manner in which they will receive and understand it best.

Doulas who are able to master this concept can be the right doula for most of the clients that inquire about their services. It is when we only communicate in our individual personality style that we find it difficult to connect with those of other styles.

The following lesson coupled with an exercise in communication will help you understand how to identify communication styles in various personalities and will teach you to speak to those individuals in a language that is most comfortable for them.

You will learn to step out of your own "communication comfort zone" and into that of the person you are communicating with. This is the first step to attunement and the one your "first impression" is based on.

Determining Personality: DISC

The DISC assessment is a four personality behavior assessment tool based on a theory developed by American psychologist William Marston.

William Marston is also the inventor of the polygraph machine, as well as the creator of the DC Comics comic book character, Wonder Woman.

Marston developed Wonder Woman out of his desire to contribute to the earliest movements of women's rights. Wonder Woman was created with the behavioral characteristics of all four personality types. She uses a lasso for truth and her heroic behaviors used to accomplish her missions show dominance, influence, security, and compliance.

His theory centers around the following four personality traits:

- Dominant – The client wants control, power, and authority.
- Influential – The client wants social interaction, praise, and recognition.
- Security Minded – The client is patient, persistent, and thoughtful.
- Compliant – The client desires structure and organization.

When you interact with clients or prospective clients it is important that they feel connected to you. By learning about DISC and how to communicate best based on personality style, your interactions will lead to a deeper level of connection.

It is important to remember that personality styles are fluid. The goal of understanding DISC is not to put people into boxes. The goal is to identify and recognize the characteristics that the individual is presenting, while being intentional about communicating in the style that best resonates with them in the moment.

Think about the people in your life that you have a difficult time communicating with. After this lesson, you may have a more clear understanding of why communication with a particular person is especially challenging for you.

Notes:

DISC

D	I	S	C
Dominant Driven Demanding Determined Decisive Delegates	Inspirational Influencing Inducing Impressive Interactive Interested in people	Supportive Submissive Stable Steady Sentimental Shy	Cautious Competent Calculating Concerned Careful Contemplative

Characteristics

Result oriented Quick decisions Need for control Power/authority Makes own rules	People oriented Love to talk Motivational Enthusiastic Recognition oriented	Family oriented Loyal Slow to change Security minded Follows rules	Detail oriented Perfectionist Critical Analytical Takes time to change

Communications

Let them talk. They will tell you what they want. They may not listen to you.	Focus on relationship building. Follow their lead. Take an interest in them. You talk most.	May not ask questions. Focus on flexibility. Ask open-ended questions.	Don't get too personal. Answer questions thoroughly. Build credibility.

Benefits Focus

You will be in total control. Nothing will happen to you without your permission. Empower them.	I will be with you the whole time. We will do this together. You're going to be amazing.	I will explain everything to you as it's happening. You will feel completely safe.	You will feel as if you have a childbirth educator with you. I will explain everything to you as it is happening. We will cover every detail.

Biggest Root Fear

Losing Control	Being judged, alone	The safety of their baby and themselves	Not understanding the process

Close the Interview

Be direct. Give them the contract and let them decide what happens next.	Share an excited compliment and express a desire to work with them.	Express your comfort level with them and offer your contract.	Give them the contract and other written information.

Exercise: Determining Personality Types

Questions: The following are actual questions written to doulas by their clients. Read through each and do your best to determine which personality styles you can decipher from each question.

1. "Thank you so much for checking in. My tough feeding journey continues…. We had success with a "dream feed" last night but the baby is still rejecting the bottle during the day, even when offered while sleepy/sleeping. We bought some bottles that were recommended for this type of situation and are hoping you have some experience with them. My supply still isn't back even though I'm nursing as much as I can. The baby is not getting enough milk because she won't take the bottle. We have tried a few virtual consults with IBCLCs but really prefer in person support. Hoping you can recommend someone good who will come to our home and help us."
2. "Hi. Somewhat urgent to receive a response ASAP. We just had our 36 week appointment with the midwives and they have ordered another growth ultrasound because my belly is still measuring small. The only availability the imaging center has this week is at 11:00 am tomorrow. Sorry for the last minute change, but is there any other time tomorrow that we can move our second prenatal to? We don't want to delay the ultrasound if possible."
3. "Good morning. Please send me your prices and information on how to book your services. We just found out that we are having a baby and I am terrified that my baby or partner could die or be harmed while giving birth."
4. "Hi there!!! We are in search of a doula for our hospital birth early next year. This is our first pregnancy, but I have heard from family members that having a doula made a big difference during labor, so we are eager to find someone in the area that might suit our needs. As you may be able to tell, we are very excited to find a doula!"
5. "Hello. We would love to set up a time to talk with you if you have availability for our due date. Before we do though, we feel it is important for the safety of our baby that the team in the room with us, including the doula, be up to date with vaccinations (flu, Covid, etc.). If this is an issue for you, we completely understand and appreciate your honesty before we consider working together. We look forward to hearing from you."
6. "Good afternoon. My apologies for the delay. Thank you for reach-

ing out so quickly. I would like to schedule our consultation, preferably in our home so that my son can also meet you. Please propose a couple of times that work for you, and we will find something that works. Thank you."
7. "Hi! I've been meaning to reach out and thank you again for all you did for our family! Our baby is about to turn 6 months old and he is the sunshine of our lives. He even makes our moody toddler smile! We are so grateful for the support and guidance you gave us. We hope all is well in your life. <3 We wish you the very best!!"
8. "I am reaching out because it was suggested to me from my lactation consultant at our pediatrician's office that you are offering services for postpartum doula support. I am interested in some help during the day and possibly someone that can help with bottle feeding my baby since he is struggling to put on weight."
9. "Hi there! I know I am late to the game, but I am hoping to find doula services for the birth of my daughter. I am due in about 5 weeks. I would love to speak with you, get to know you, and discuss options for availability! Thanks!"
10. "Updating you that I officially switched to Dr. Z. I feel good about switching for a lot of reasons, but I think one interaction really exemplifies it. I shared with him how I've been feeling and some of the things I've been nervous about, and he asked 'What will make you feel better?' His bedside manner was a night and day difference from Dr. A."

Notes:

Contributing Factors to Negativity Around Birth

As a pregnant family plans for the birth of their child, a positive labor experience is typically one of the goals. However, birth is unpredictable and the outcome does not always meet the expectation. There are several other factors that can contribute to a less than positive birth experience. Fear, anxiety, previous birth trauma, poor medical treatment, and the impact of medical and systemic racism are some of the things that can shape childbirth. As doulas, it is important to acknowledge these complications and the impact they may have on your clients.

Birth Trauma

Birth trauma refers to any physical or emotional distress experienced by the birthing person during or immediately after childbirth. Any event that is experienced or witnessed as traumatic can leave a lasting impact on the person. In the realm of childbirth, trauma is often the result of an individual fearing for their life and/or the life of their child during labor or childbirth. Losing control of bodily autonomy, lack of informed consent when it comes to medical decisions, or being treated without respect or dignity during labor can also result in birth trauma for the individual.

A recent National Institute of Health study found that anywhere between 20% and 47% of birthing persons report some kind of traumatic event during labor and delivery. These numbers reinforce that birth trauma is not a rare occurrence.
(Source: Traumatic Childbirth and Birth Related Post-Traumatic Stress Disorder in the Time of the Covid-19 Pandemic: A Prospective Cohort Study, 2022)

There is no all encompassing definition of a traumatic birth. Two people can experience the same situation and process them in completely opposite ways. As doulas, it is not appropriate to label a client's birth as "traumatic" or "not traumatic." We must be sensitive to our client's perceptions of their birth. If any part of their birth feels traumatic to them, they have experienced birth trauma.

As a doula, you can also experience trauma when you are exposed to another person's difficult birth experience. This is referred to as secondary trauma. Just as you would not minimize or dismiss a client's trauma, do not minimize your own. It is necessary for you to address this secondary trauma by processing it with a trusted colleague or mentor and/or by seeking therapeutic relief.

Obstetrical Violence/Systemic Bias/Medical Racism

Another issue that can affect the birth experience for individuals is the medical treatment the laboring person receives. In 2023, the CDC released a study that found that 20% of birthing persons surveyed experienced some form of medical mistreatment during their pregnancy and/or delivery. That number was higher for black (30%), hispanic (29%), and multiracial (27%) individuals. Medical mistreatment was also reported to be higher among birthing individuals that had no insurance (28%) or had public insurance (26%).

(Source: CDC Vital Signs August 2023)

The mistreatment reported included medical providers not responding to requests for help, them shouting at or scolding patients, not protecting the patients' physical privacy, and withholding medical treatment or making patients accept unwanted treatment.

Many birthing individuals in the United States experience medical racism. According to the study mentioned above, 40% of black individuals reported discrimination during their birth from a medical provider. Hispanic persons and multiracial persons reported higher levels of discrimination than their white counterparts - 39% and 37% respectively.

Determining why these statistics are what they are is not simple, however, the understanding lies in acknowledging the systemic racism that exists within our hospital/medical systems. Even though medical professionals have a duty to treat all patients with equal care, the history of black experimentation, segregated medical care, and white privilege continue to influence the overall care that non-white populations receive in this country.

(Source: Structural Racism and Supporting Black Lives, Rachel R. Hardeman et. al. - 12/2016)

Even today, medical textbooks do not accurately represent signs, symptoms, and diagnoses across races; instead catering the majority of imagery to white patients.

(Source: Racism and medical education | Shujhat Khan, Areeb Mian | September, 2020)

These examples of bias disproportionately affect BIPOC communities, who can be under- or mis-diagnosed based on the medical provider's lack of understanding of how medical issues can present across races. Examples of implicit bias show themselves in long-held, but completely false, beliefs that black individuals have higher pain thresholds and/or that their blood

coagulates more quickly than white individuals.
(Source: Racial bias in pain assessment and treatment recommendations, and false beliefs about biological differences between blacks and whites | Kelly M. Hoffman | April 2016)

All of this works against non-white patients in a medical system that is still predominantly served by white providers.

Maternal and Infant Mortality Rates

Another alarming statistic related to birth in this country are the rates of maternal mortality. A 2021 CDC study reports that the maternal mortality rate continues to rise in the United States. In 2019, 20.1 deaths were reported per 100,000 births, however in 2021 that number had risen to 32.9 deaths per 100,000 births.
(Source: Maternal Mortality Rates in the United States, Donna L. Hoyert, CDC 2021)

The United States ranks among the highest for maternal mortality rates among developed countries. Global experts point to the lack of widespread models of midwifery care and the lack of frequent and available postpartum medical care.
(Source: Maternal Mortality and Maternity Care in the United States Compared to 10 Other Developed Countries, The Commonwealth Fund | November 2020)

These numbers are even higher for black individuals at 69.9 deaths per 100,000 births, which is over 2.5 times higher than their white counterparts. The CDC classified this increase as "significant."
(Source: Maternal Mortality Rates in the United States, Donna L. Hoyert, CDC 2021)

Although infant mortality rates have begun to decline over the past few years, the United States still remains amongst the top of high-income countries worldwide when it comes to infant mortality rates.
(Source: US Has Highest Infant, Maternal Mortality Rates Despite the Most Health Care Spending, Justina Petrullo | January 2023)

In 2021, the CDC reported 5.4 deaths per 1000 live births. For black infants that number was 10.6 deaths per 1000 live births, which is nearly double their white counterparts.
(Source: Infant Mortality in the United States, 2021: Data From the Period Linked Birth/Infant Death File)

All of these statistics can weigh heavily on the pregnant person. As a birthworker in this country we must acknowledge these issues and understand how they shape the birth experience for our clients. Doulas cannot bear the burden of the realities of the American healthcare system. However, by recognizing them, and working toward changing them, a doula can help empower and support their clients as they advocate for the care they are entitled to in an effort to achieve a safe and positive birth.

Birth Philosophies

What is a philosophy?

phi·los·o·phy n. pl. phi·los·o·phies

1. Love and pursuit of wisdom by intellectual means and moral self-discipline.
2. Investigation of the nature, causes, or principles of reality, knowledge, or values, based on logical reasoning rather than empirical methods.
3. A system of thought based on or involving such inquiry.
4. The critical analysis of fundamental assumptions or beliefs.

Individuals who seek out the support of a labor doula have often invested a great amount of time in developing a philosophy surrounding birth. They have read, researched, asked questions, witnessed birth, etc. These inquiries and experiences are what lead us to a personal philosophy.

It is extremely important that doulas, as support people, check their own philosophies at the door, so to speak. We all have personal philosophies and as doulas, we are certainly "invested" in birth. For many of us, we are called to this line of work but it is crucial to our clients that we bring NON-JUDGMENTAL support to them. Differences between our personal birth philosophies and theirs can cause conflict for them regarding our ability to provide them with support. They are entitled to our unbiased support and must feel as though they will receive it.

Overview of Main Birth Philosophies

Although there are many variations of birthing philosophies, creating a dialogue with your client to obtain an understanding of their general birth philosophy is very important. From this information, you will be able to validate, encourage, and contribute to each client's support and empowerment.

Completely Unmedicated

This philosophy is based on the idea that birth is a normal, natural event in a person's life; that their body is designed to birth the baby that grows within it. This client will likely be interested in birthing at home either with a homebirth midwife or, in some cases, choosing to have an unassisted birth. The other options that suit this philosophy are a birth center or a birth-friendly hospital assisted by a Certified Nurse Midwife and a doula.

*A ProDoula will not attend intentionally, unassisted births.

Unmedicated With Medical Support Close By

This philosophy is based on the idea that the client is very comfortable with unmedicated birth. Either they or their partner feel more confident birthing in a hospital than at home. One or both of them take comfort in knowing that if they need or desire a medical intervention, they are in a place that will meet those requests swiftly. This client is likely expressing that they would like to have an unmedicated birth but, if they decide that they would like an epidural, they expect their team's full support.

Medical With an Open-Mindedness to Surgical

This philosophy is based on the idea that the client is putting their faith and trust in their medical providers. They believe that the physician and nursing staff are the experts and they take comfort in knowing that they will keep them and their baby safe.

What Do Our Clients Believe?

We must understand our clients' beliefs surrounding birth. These beliefs are personal and they are the very reason that someone may desire the support of a doula. The client believes that the doula's support will reduce their fear while instilling strength in them and enabling their empowerment.

Doulas lift clients up and support them during pregnancy and birth, but, most importantly, a doula helps their client feel good about their body, their birth, and their decisions. For this reason, one of the roles of a doula is to nurture and affirm the client while they search to find their personal birth philosophy. The doula validates and encourages the dialogue that helps the client arrive at their conclusions.

A doula asks thought-provoking questions and provides resources and evidence-based information that supports the client's desires. A doula praises the client for being true to themselves and provides the client with a positive place to explore all of the birth options available to them.
It is important to understand the client's philosophy regarding birth

before assisting them in organizing their birth plan. To best support each client, it is essential that you understand the things that matter most to them. As a doula, you will come to learn about the routine protocols of the birth facilities in your area. This will enable you to answer the following questions and more:

- If they choose water-birth, does the facility support water-birth?
- If they oppose induction, how far past their due date will their provider be comfortable with them going?
- If they want to ambulate during labor, does the facility support intermittent fetal monitoring or use telemetry for monitoring?
- If they are opposed to IV fluids, does the facility use routine IV hydration or can that be refused?

A personal birth philosophy comes from an individual's unique vision for their birth. How they answer the following questions will help determine their personal philosophy:

- How do they feel about the process of birth:
  - Excited?
  - Fearful?
  - Safe?
  - Sacred?
- Do they feel it is a natural process or a dangerous one?
- Do they want medical interventions available to them during the process?
- Do they want a birth experience with little to no intervention?
- Do they feel called to birth in the water?
- Who do they imagine being in attendance during their birth?
- Do they have any religious or cultural ceremonies that they would like incorporated into their birth experience?

Once a client has asked themselves these questions and they and their partner determine their wishes, then they are ready to make decisions about the maternity care that is right for them.

As their doula, you will want to learn the answers to these questions as well. This will enable you to support their decisions and direct them to the best possible resources available. It is also important to encourage your clients to be open minded if or when their birth plans must change due to a medical emergency.

Understanding the Birth Environment

The DISC Assessment and the Labor Room

Bringing your new understanding of communication styles to the birth will be important for you and advantageous to your client.

You now have the ability to quickly assess the communication styles of the medical providers that are caring for your client. Work mindfully to speak to them in the language that is most comfortable for each person in order to facilitate a positive connection between you and the entire birth team. By doing this you will help create a more comfortable environment which will have a positive impact on your client's birth experience and your ability to expand your network.

Universal Precautions for Birth Workers

Regardless of where your client decides to give birth, as a doula it is extremely important to understand and follow Universal Precautions for birth workers. Developed by the Centers for Disease Control in 1985, Universal Precautions are a set of guidelines to prevent those exposed to blood and other bodily fluids from bloodborne pathogens.

In your role as a labor doula, the vaginal secretions of the birthing person such as bloody show, amniotic fluid, and any other bodily fluid that is visibly contaminated with blood or may contain blood are considered potentially infectious.

According to the CDC:

> - *Standard precautions apply to the care of all patients, irrespective of their disease state. These precautions apply when there is a risk of potential exposure to (1) blood; (2) all body fluids, secretions, and excretions, except sweat, regardless of whether or not they contain visible blood; (3) non-intact skin; and (4) mucous membranes. This includes hand hygiene and personal protective equipment (PPE), with hand hygiene being the single most important means to prevent transmission of disease.*
> *(Source: Universal Precautions: Ian M. Broussard; Chadi I. Kahwaji, July 2023)*

The most commonly recommended precautions that apply to doulas is as follows, before and after direct contact:

- Handwashing for at least 40-60 seconds
- Hand rubbing with alcohol (hand sanitizer) that completely covers hands and rubbed until dry
- Gloves must be worn when touching body parts or items exposed to bodily fluids
  - When helping change chux pads, sheets, soiled clothing items, etc.
  - When touching body parts exposed to vaginal secretions, bloody show, amniotic fluids, or blood
    - Gloves should be changed after touching any of the above, hands washed, and a fresh pair put on before touching clean surfaces, other items, or the client's body parts

It is important to remember that the baby is covered in vaginal secretions, amniotic fluid, and maternal blood. Gloves should be utilized when handling the newborn, when assisting with breastfeeding, or other newborn care until the infant has been appropriately bathed.

Birth Settings

Home Birth

According to the National Vital Statistics Report from November 2022:

- There was a 12% increase in home births from 2020 to 2021 following a 22% increase from 2019 to 2020, with increases by maternal race and Hispanic origin ranging from 21%-36%.
- The percentage of home births for all U.S. birthing individuals increased between 2020 and 2021 for most months, peaking in January 2021 at 1.51%.
- From 2020 to 2021, the percentage of home births increased in 30 states, with increases ranging from 8% for Florida to 49% for West Virginia.
- There were 51,642 home births in 2021, an increase of 13% from 2020 (45,646). This increase followed a 19% rise in the number of home births from 2019 (38,506) to 2020.
- For (non-Hispanic) White birthing persons, the percentage of home births increased 10%, from about 1.9% of all births in 2020 to almost 2.1% in 2021. This followed a 21% increase from 2019 (1.55%) to 2020.
- Home births among (non-Hispanic) Black individuals increased 21%, from 0.68% to 0.82% of all births from 2020 to 2021. The

percentage of home births increased 36% from 2019 (0.50%) to 2020.
- For Hispanic birthing persons, home births increased from 0.48% in 2020 to 0.55% in 2021, an increase of 15%. The percentage of home births increased 30% from 2019 (0.37%) to 2020.

(Source: National Vital Statistics Reports | Volume 71, Number 8 November 17, 2022)

While it is legal to choose to give birth at home in all 50 states, regulations that oversee midwifery care limit access to care in some states. For more information about the legality of homebirth midwifery on a state-by-state basis visit: https://mana.org/about-midwives/state-by-state

Generally, birth at home makes for a very relaxed environment. It is assumed by the birthing individual that birth is natural and being home, nurtured by loved ones with the help of a doula and midwife, helps normalize this idea. As a doula, during a home birth consider utilizing all of the tools a home offers to the client. Additionally, consider incorporating comfort measures that include the 5 senses: lighting, scents, music, touch, and tastes.

- Lighting can have a big impact on the client's oxytocin levels, so it is important to keep the lighting calm and relaxed.
- The sense of smell is closely related to our memory. Lighting candles with scents that are pleasing to the client can enhance the experience.
- Some clients will prepare their own playlists. Music that is familiar to them can enhance their level of comfort and relaxation.
- During labor, stroking, light massage, and counter pressure are often used to relax the client and relieve pain. Showers and tubs are also beneficial for labor and/or delivery.
- Encourage the client to have their preferred snacks and drinks available at home during labor.

Birth at home also means utilizing other areas of the home during the labor process. The bed for resting and other labor positions, stairs for walking/lunging and moving the pelvis, kitchen for nutrition and hydration, the front porch for a change of scenery and fresh air, etc.

While the birth tub will likely be set up in a chosen room, that does not mean that the rest of the home is off-limits. In fact, sometimes the room can begin to feel stale. A change of space can increase energy levels and contribute positively to the labor process.

After the birth, it is expected that you will stay a little bit longer than you might at a hospital birth. You may offer assistance with infant feeding, by tidying up the birth space, preparing a snack for the client, changing the linens on the bed, etc.

Routine Protocols in the Home Birth Setting

In a home birth setting, state laws regulating midwifery will determine practice protocols that midwives must follow. These protocols typically include:

- Assessment of the birthing person's vitals at regular intervals
- Assessment of the fetal heart tones at regular intervals
- Practice guidelines typically include guidance for developments during labor that necessitate a transfer of care to a hospital

Hospital Birth

In the United States the majority of infants are born in the hospital setting. In some communities, in-hospital birth centers account for an undetermined percentage of births attended by midwives or other obstetrical care providers. These births are often listed as hospital births even though they may occur in the birth center portion of the facility.

When attending a hospital birth, there are several environmental factors that a doula should be aware of.

The labor and delivery nurse – A labor and delivery nurse typically works 12-hour shifts, three to four times a week. Be sure to introduce yourself as the doula, while also being mindful of their role and responsibilities. Always let the nurse know that you are there to help, and if there is anything you can do to assist, to just ask. A positive interaction between you and the nurse will be beneficial to your client.

The medical equipment – All of the medical equipment in the labor room is "hands-off" for doulas unless a medical professional asks for assistance.

Materials – Make sure you know where you can find all of the things you may need during the birth. Chux pads, towels, blankets, gowns, face cloths, basins (for ice water or vomit), pads, underwear, etc. Look around the room and make a mental note of things you are not able to find. If you need these items, ask the nurse for them when they return to the room.

Your things – Make sure all of your belongings (and your client's belongings) are neatly tucked out of the way. Bags, purses, birth balls, etc. In the event of an emergency, the path in and out of the room must be clear.

Lights – Make sure you know where the light switches are so that you can easily turn them off and on. Also note where the thermostat is in the room and find out if you are able to control it.

Stay out of the way – There is a small amount of space on either side of the bed. Make sure the provider or nurse has full access to the patient when necessary.

Fetal monitors – The fetal monitor measures the length and frequency of contractions and the baby's heart rate. If the client is moving or sitting, it may be difficult to pick up the baby's fetal heart tones with the monitor.

There may be times when the client is asked to lay on the bed in order to get an accurate account of the baby's heart rate.

Find the kitchen – Know where the cups, straws, juice, ice, etc. are stored. Be sure to ask the client's partner if they need anything when you are going to the kitchen (coffee, snack, etc.). Do not eat food that has a strong smell as a client's sense of smell may be heightened during labor and it could cause them to become nauseous. Before others eat in the room, ask the client if it will bother them. After delivery, if the cafeteria is open, ask if a meal can be ordered for the client. Clients are typically very hungry after delivery.

Do not eat in front of the client if they are not permitted to eat.

Do a run-through – If you are not familiar with the hospital, it is a good idea to go there for a tour to learn as much as you can about the parking, elevators, check-in process, the labor unit, etc. You do not want to be learning about these things at 3:00am the day of the client's delivery. The more you know, the more comfortable your client will be having you by their side.

Routine Protocols in the Hospital Setting

While routine hospital protocols will vary from location to location there are some common protocols that exist in the majority of locations.

The following are a list of common hospital protocols:

- Monitoring of the birthing person's vitals upon admission and for the duration of the hospital stay
    - A vaginal exam may be performed before the birthing person is admitted to the hospital during labor
- Monitoring and assessment of the fetal heartbeat upon admission and through labor, either in a continuous or intermittent manner
- Reviewing or taking the birthing person's medical and psycho-social history at admission
- Insertion of a saline lock or an IV catheter
- Restrictions on eating and drinking during labor is common in many facilities
- Protocols surrounding when interventions such as augmentation of labor should be recommended are typically a part of the facilities practice guidelines for providers; however, these vary from

In 2011, the Consortium for Safe Labor officially redefined active labor as beginning at 6cm, not at 4cm as defined previously by obstetrician Emanuel Friedman, who is discussed more below.

"The Consortium on Safe Labor data highlight two important features of contemporary labor progress (Fig. 4). First, from 4–6 cm, nulliparous and multiparous [individuals] dilated at essentially the same rate, and more slowly than historically described. Beyond 6 cm, multiparous [individuals] dilated more rapidly. Second, the maximal slope in the rate of change of cervical dilation over time (ie, the active phase) often did not start until at least 6 cm. The Consortium on Safe Labor data do not directly address an optimal duration for the diagnosis of active phase protraction or labor arrest, but do suggest that neither should be diagnosed before 6 cm of dilation. Because they are contemporary and robust, it seems that the Consortium on Safe Labor data, rather than the standards proposed by Friedman, should inform evidence-based labor management."

(Source: ACOG Committee Opinion | Number 766 | February 2019)

Friedman's Curve

Emanuel Friedman is a retired American obstetrician. He is best known for his work out of Columbia University in 1955. The focus of this study was to determine how long it took for the cervix to dilate one centimeter during labor. His study observed 500 white, first time birthing individuals at one hospital. Dr. Friedman plotted his results from these 500 labors onto a graph and calculated the average length of time it took for the cervix to dilate one centimeter.

Before Dr. Friedman's study was published, doctors in the United States had only performed studies on the average length of labor, looking only at the overall length, versus the time it took for the cervix to progress centimeter by centimeter.

Once published in 1955, Friedman's Curve became the gold standard of care in determining if a labor was progressing at an optimal pace. When a labor pattern deviates from the "curve," interventions are implemented to try and get the labor back on course.

In 2012, changemakers in obstetrics convened with the focus of "Preventing the Primary Cesarean." This workshop produced a consensus statement in 2014 from ACOG titled "Safe Prevention of the Primary Cesarean Delivery," which redefined the markers for normal and abnormal labor, effectively casting Friedman's Curve aside.

While many providers have adopted the new standards for the pace of normal and abnormal labor, the change wasn't without resistance by some providers. It is possible that you may see Friedman's Curve still being used in your community. In such cases, helping clients learn about the new standards and helping them formulate questions to ask their provider about their approach is beneficial.

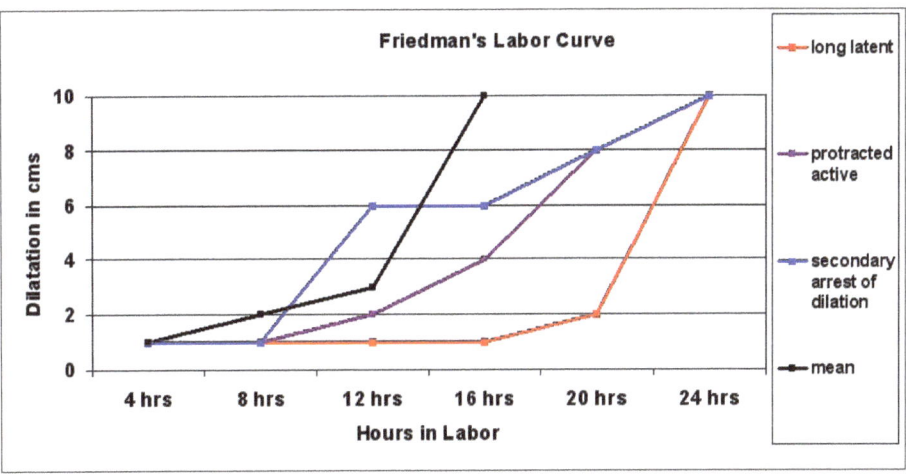

Patient's Bill of Rights

According to the U.S. Department of Health & Human Services, a patient in a medical establishment has certain rights. Some rights are dictated from the federal level, others will be dictated from the state level. Each hospital will also have a version of their own Patient's Bill of Rights. It is recommended that you familiarize yourself with these rights for each hospital that you will be attending births at.

Two of the most important rights that your clients have are the right to informed consent and the right of refusal.

Informed consent means that a patient has the right to be informed about their medical condition which includes the risks and benefits of treatment and any available alternatives. Patients also have the right to refuse any suggested course of treatment or intervention, even if it is recommended by their provider.

In most hospitals in the United States, a patient is expected to sign a general consent to treat upon admission. While a client has the right to informed consent, this general consent to treat allows the provider to treat the patient to the standard of care for the condition they are presenting with.

Birth - It's a Hormonal Process

While most of the focus is placed on the physical process of labor and birth, what often goes unnoticed is that the initiation and continuation of labor is a fundamentally hormonal process.

The spontaneous onset of labor is initiated by a sequence of hormonal changes.

Prostaglandins

Before the uterus can begin to produce progressive contractions, a sequence of hormonal changes must be initiated. This process begins with the release of prostaglandins which are hormone-like substances that affect several bodily functions including uterine contractions. Prostaglandins are found in the uterine lining of the pregnant person and in the fetal membranes.

The uterus is lined with oxytocin receptors. During pregnancy the hormone progesterone blocks the oxytocin receptors from utilizing circulating oxytocin to keep the uterus relaxed. However, near the end of pregnancy prostaglandin levels will rise to aid in the cervical ripening process and to open the oxytocin receptors of the uterus. This will allow the uterus to utilize the circulating oxytocin to produce progressive contractions.

Prostaglandins come first. If they are not in place none of the ways to "bring on" labor will be effective. For this reason, cervical ripening methods like Cervidil or Cytotec are typically used to increase the chances of a successful induction of labor and vaginal birth.

Prostaglandins are found in semen, evening primrose oil, and castor oil. This is why providers may recommend sex with ejaculation for those hoping to begin labor. In addition, the prostaglandins found in evening primrose oil and castor oil can lead some providers, most often midwives, to recommend their use for cervical ripening at the end of pregnancy.

Oxytocin

Oxytocin is widely known as the hormone of love. It is also known as the hormone of labor. It is responsible for uterine contractions and it stimulates nurturing and loving feelings that enable bonding.

Oxytocin is released from the pituitary gland in the brain. During labor and birth it is released in pulses.

The oxytocin receptor sites that line the uterus pick up the oxytocin being released from the pituitary. The smooth muscle fibers of the uterus that are now online as a result of prostaglandins pick up the circulating oxytocin and begin to contract together. This creates a contraction pattern that typically results in active labor.

Adrenaline

Adrenaline is known as the "fight or flight" hormone. It can play a huge role during labor. It is released in response to stress, fear, and/or extreme pain. When an individual feels fearful or anxious during labor, they release adrenaline which suppresses the release of oxytocin. Utilizing verbal affirmations as well as other comforting techniques can be extremely beneficial to keeping the client relaxed and aiding in the flow of oxytocin.

Endorphins

Endorphins, or beta-endorphins, are known as the body's natural pain killers. They are natural occurring opiates that have properties similar to demerol or morphine. Endorphins come from the pituitary gland in the brain. During sex, pregnancy, birth, and breastfeeding high levels are present. While in labor, endorphins contribute to a decreased perception of pain for the birthing person. They also prepare the newborn for breathing outside of the uterus and regulate the newborn's temperature.

High levels of endorphins during labor create an environment in the brain that enables the laboring person to bond quickly and easily. The bond that a birthing person can form with their nurse during labor is a great example of this. It also primes the client's brain to bond more deeply with their doula during the process.

Supporting Labor

Emotional Support

Emotional support is best described as the ability to connect with another person by having a sensitive and understanding approach to their needs and feelings. When we are successful in providing emotional support, our clients can best share their fears, anxieties, desires, and emotions with us. For our clients, being able to communicate these thoughts enables them to process and release emotions which can bring them comfort, relaxation, and confidence while giving them the ability to continue laboring.

It is best said that the primary focus of doctors, midwives, and nurses is "healthy baby/healthy parent," while the primary focus of the doula is "healthy bond/healthy mind."

Provide encouragement, reassurance, and a non-judgmental attitude towards your client to support their emotional relaxation. Clear your mind of any personal agendas you may have in order to be their "sounding board" and provide them with the nurturing emotional support that will best serve them.

When speaking with clients, avoid comments like:

- Don't worry
- Just relax
- You're fine

These comments can feel condescending to clients as well as make them feel unheard. If they had the ability not to worry, they wouldn't be worried.

Instead, make them comfortable by helping them understand that it is normal to have overwhelming rushes of emotions, thoughts, and concerns during this highly transitional experience. As the doula, never forget how vulnerable your client is during this time. Focus on being sympathetic, compassionate, and, of course, non-judgmental as you support your client.

Educational Support

Educational support refers to the base of knowledge that you must obtain to adequately support your client through labor. Through this training and your comprehensive open book certification exam, you will acquire the knowledge and skills to provide an exceptional level of informational support to your client during pregnancy, birth, and in the early postpartum hours.

It is important to remember that each client decides what they want to learn. What information a client may be interested in is often rooted in their personality style. The C personality will likely want more resources and evidence-based information than the S personality. The I personality may rely more on the opinions of friends, family members, or trusted professionals to make decisions. The D personality will likely be direct and decisive about what they want to know.

However, there are an infinite number of scenarios and situations that can occur during pregnancy and birth. If at any time you are asked a question or for information that you are not certain of, it is not only appropriate but preferred that you answer by saying, "I am not certain of the answer, but I have the resources I need to get you an answer as soon as possible." It is not reasonable to expect you to know everything regarding medical conditions or procedures. Although it is expected that you have the ability to acquire a resource to help your client understand information they are given. This is why it is imperative that you stay current on the latest evidence-based information and pursue on-going education.

Physical Support

Touching your client with confidence is key to their physical and emotional comfort during labor. Touch in the form of holding, massage, stroking, and soothing is both comforting and nurturing and it plays a huge role in labor support.

Knowing how and when to touch are equally important, so practicing at home with a partner can be extremely valuable. Consider working towards becoming a more "physical person" in your day-to-day life to help you develop your confidence with touch.

Physical support includes but is not limited to:

- Massage/counter-pressure
- Cleaning/wiping personal areas (with gloves)
- Nipple stimulation
- Hugging/holding
- Hair brushing

- Position changes
- Reminders to eat, drink, or urinate

Notes:

Cervical Changes During Childbirth

In order for the baby to pass through the vagina and be born, it must find its way through the cervix. A normal, closed cervix feels much like the tip of your nose. When it is fully dilated and effaced (ready for delivery), it feels more like the skin between your thumb and index finger when they are fully extended.

The cervix must do four things in order to prepare for the birth of the baby. There is no particular order to these changes. Although the four changes are numbered, there is no expectation for them to happen in the order listed.

1. The cervix must move from the posterior position (pointing toward the back of the body) to the anterior position (pointing toward the front of the body).
2. The cervix must ripen or become soft. Associated with cervical ripening is an increase in the enzyme cyclooxygenase-2, leading to a local increase of prostaglandin in the cervix.
3. The cervix must efface or become thin. As the uterus contracts, the extended tightening of it causes the cervix to thin out or efface.
4. The cervix must dilate or open. It must open to 10cm of dilation in order for the baby to pass through it and enter into the vagina. Long, strong, and frequent contractions accompanied by the pressure of the baby's head against the cervix cause it to dilate completely.

All four of these phases occur during the first stage of labor. During a vaginal exam, the provider is also checking the baby's position in relation to the pelvis. This is referred to as the baby's station.

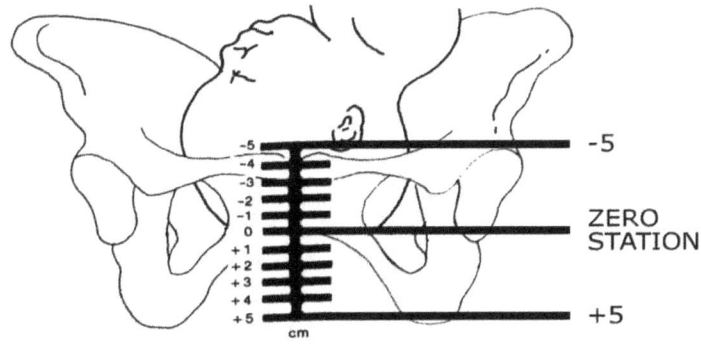

The spines on either side of the pelvis indicate 0 station. When the fetal head is higher than those spines, the station is considered a negative station and is described as -1, -2, -3, or -4 station. When the fetal head is lower than the spines, the station is considered a positive station and is described as +1, +2, +3, or +4 station.

The Cervix is NOT the Only Indication of Labor Progress

In fact, it can often be misleading and a huge distraction for the client. During some labors, the client may show all the signs of being in transition only to have an exam and find out the cervix is just 5-6cm dilated.

This can be very disappointing for the client. Use verbal affirmations to encourage them to keep going and to stay positive. Let them know that the labor says the client is further along than the cervix shows and the two will catch up soon.

Sometimes the cervix has to catch up with the labor and sometimes the labor has to catch up with the cervix.

Stay positive and acknowledge all of the changes.

- You are making so much progress
- Your contractions are longer, stronger, and closer together
- Your body IS making all of the necessary changes
- Your baby has moved down
- Your cervix IS opening

The Mucus Plug

Mucus that accumulates at the cervix during pregnancy is referred to as the "mucus plug." When the cervix begins to soften and open, the mucus is released into the vagina and expelled. It may appear to be clear, pink, brown, or slightly blood-tinged. Once released, labor may begin within a day or two OR within a week or two. While the release of the mucus plug is no indication of when labor will begin, it is a positive sign of cervical change.

Stages of Labor

There are three stages of labor:

- First stage - The time of the onset of true labor through the cervix becoming completely dilated.
- Second stage - The period between when the cervix is completely dilated and when the baby is delivered. Also known as the pushing phase.
- Third stage - The delivery of the placenta.

First Stage

- Labor in this unit is divided into the three phases of the first stage of labor: early labor, active labor, and transitional labor.

Early Labor

The first phase of labor, or "early labor," is considered to be when the client is experiencing fairly regular contractions that are causing cervical change. These changes would include the cervix beginning to soften (efface) and open (dilate). Early labor ends when the cervix is about 6 centimeters dilated and there is an acceleration in the labor. A person who is giving birth for the first time (primipara) can expect this stage to last anywhere from 12-24 hours.

- *Anatomy* - In early labor, the cervix is softening (ripening), thinning (effacing), opening (dilating), and moving from the posterior position (pointing towards the client's back) to the anterior position (pointing towards the client's front).
- *Signs and symptoms* - The signs and symptoms that will likely accompany this stage of labor are mild to moderate, regular or irregular contractions lasting between 30-60 seconds. The client typically feels calm and "normal" during this time. Many clients are not sure that they are experiencing contractions during this time and often report feeling "crampy." For some, prior to early labor or during it, a client may see a mass or secretion of brown or blood-tinged mucus from the vagina known as the mucus plug. They may also experience loose or soft bowel movements during this time. Other symptoms may include nausea and emotional responses. For most clients, this is not an uncomfortable time but a time filled with unanswered questions. Speaking to their doula periodically

during early labor helps a client to relax and enable the process of labor to continue.
- **Comfort measures** - Encouraging a client to try their best to "ignore" these signs and symptoms for as long as they are able will help them to manage this period of labor. Walking, resting, cooking, going to the movies, or visiting with a friend can all be great distractions. Remind clients in early labor to eat when they are hungry, drink when they are thirsty, and rest when they are tired. This is a special time for a client and they don't usually require your physical support at this time. Being available to give information and reassurance during this time is extremely valuable to the client and their partner. It is a celebration for them of their last day or two as a couple, before they become a family, and they will likely enjoy their time alone for now.

Active Labor

The second phase of labor, or "active labor," is the period of time when the cervix dilates from about 6 to 8 centimeters. Contractions during this time are typically regular. They are likely between 3-5 minutes apart and lasting about 60 seconds. A person who is giving birth for the first time can expect this stage of labor to last between 6-10 hours. Upon approaching active labor, the client's mood and overall body language will likely change. They will become more focused and be less interested in joking or chatting.

- **Anatomy** - During active labor, the cervix is continuing to soften (efface) and open (dilate). The contractions of the uterus are becoming longer, stronger, and closer together. They are lasting between 60-90 seconds and are requiring a great deal of concentration to manage them.
- **Signs and symptoms** - The client's legs may cramp and they may begin to feel nausea, low back pain, shaking, and emotionality. The client's hormone levels are changing rapidly and they may experience what seems like "the chills" during this time. Although they are not cold, they appear to be shivering to the point of teeth chattering. This is a normal reaction to the changes occurring during labor.
- **Comfort measures** - During active labor the client usually requires more physical and emotional support. It is likely that they will want the doula to be with them during this time. Comfort measures include position changes, massage, counter-pressure, slow

deep breathing, ice/heat, relaxation/meditation, or shower or bath. During this time the client often prefers no distractions. It is respectful of those present to "match the mood" and allow the laboring person the uninterrupted ability to stay completely focused. Questions that require more than a yes or no answer can be very distracting. Support through information is expected from you as the doula. The client should be encouraged to relax and recover between each contraction in order to allow the labor to progress and not cause them to become exhausted. Offering ice chips or sips of water after each contraction will help to keep the client well hydrated.

Rituals Associated With Labor

Ritual - rit•u•al

1. done as part of a ceremony or ritual
2. always done in a particular situation and in the same way each time

Easily recognized rituals during labor are breathing and movement. Most individuals instinctively fall into a patterned style of breathing during labor. It is quite common to observe repetitive movements during the labor process that are ritualistic as well. Swaying from side to side, rocking on a birth ball, or moving into a certain position as a contraction begins.

According to emerging research out of UC Berkeley, rituals serve to regulate emotions, performance goal states, and foster social connections. Rituals create feelings of control and order during times of anxiety or uncertainty.

"Clinical studies provide relatively strong support that rituals regulate negative emotions, because they demonstrate that rituals are more likely to emerge when performers experience an emotional deficit—that is, an emotional state that diverges from one's desired state."
 The Psychology of Rituals: An Integrative Review and Process-Based Framework: 2017

This research supports that when utilizing a ritual to successfully move through contractions, the brain conveys that the success of the ritual for the previous contraction will likely yield similar results when used again. These rituals can lead to birthing individuals feeling more in control of the experience and will likely reduce their level of anxiety and fear.

Labor and birth are instinctual and so are some of the rituals that clients connect with it. It is important that we do not interfere with these rituals as they are part of the "flow" of that client's labor. These rituals can reveal themselves in a number of ways as the contraction begins, peaks, and ends.

- A hand motion
- A tapping or drumming
- Rubbing of legs
- Repeating a phrase or word
- Nodding of their head
- Rocking
- Breathing patterns
- And more

Gently remind your client's partner not to interfere with this or bring the client's attention to the ritual as they may feel inhibited by others acknowledging it. Part of your role is to hold this sacred space for the client and they are counting on you to do this.

Assertive/Accommodating Approach

Labor support is often a combination of accommodation and assertion. Sometimes the client leads the labor and sometimes they look to the doula to lead them. As a doula, you must recognize what they need, when they need it, and be prepared to shift gears as their needs change.

Assertive

1. Confident and direct in claiming one's rights or putting forward one's views
2. Given to making assertions or bold demands; dogmatic or aggressive

Accommodate

1. To do a favor or service for; oblige
2. To provide for; supply with
3. To hold comfortably without crowding
4. To make suitable; adapt
5. To allow for; consider

Occasionally during a difficult part of labor, your client may lose their rhythm. They may become frantic and need your assertive approach to help them refocus. In this scenario be assertive, yet kind and compassionate. Place your hands on the client and position yourself face-to-face with them. Tell your client to open their eyes and look at you. Look into their eyes and tell them, "We will do this together," "Breathe with me," "Deep breath in (do it yourself) and exhale (long and slow with vocalization) OOOOOOHH," "And breathe in (again, do it with them) and exhale, OOOOOOHH." Do this until the contraction subsides and then offer gentle but confident affirmation.

- "Great job!"
- "We'll do this one contraction at a time."
- "We'll do it together."
- "You're doing great!"
- "This is exactly what I would expect to see during this part of labor."

Transitional Labor

This third phase of labor is typically the shortest but most intense part of labor. Clients benefit from a great deal of physical, educational, and emotional support from their birth team during this time. Those giving birth for the first time can expect this phase to last 30 minutes to 4+ hours.

- *Anatomy* - The cervix of a client who is in transitional labor is between 8-10 centimeters dilated. Long, strong, and closely spaced contractions are causing the cervix to become completely thinned out (100% effaced), and open (dilating) to 10 centimeters during this time. These contractions are lasting about 90 seconds and coming about 2 minutes apart. These long, strong, and closely spaced uterine contractions are moving the baby down lower into the pelvis in preparation for birth.
- *Signs and symptoms* - The signs or symptoms of transitional labor may include bloody/mucus discharge, very intense contractions, low back pain, self-doubt, shakes or what appears to be "the chills," rapid body temperature changes (hot to cold/cold to hot), leg cramps, exhaustion, and more. Periodically during transition, some clients may feel the need to move their bowels or bear down. Often it is the pressure from the baby moving down that is triggering this sensation. Encouraging the client to try to use the toilet during this time is validating and allows them to understand this sensation more clearly. The client may question their ability

to continue during this phase and may begin to reconsider their plans in regard to pain management.
- **Comfort measures** - During transitional labor many clients require a great deal of physical support. During contractions you can help comfort the client with counter-pressure, face-to-face/eye-to-eye breathing, verbal affirmations, vocalization, and more. Remember, they are working extremely hard through this phase and may be feeling hot and thirsty. Offer ice or water after each contraction and have an ice bath and washcloths ready to cool the client down as each contraction passes. Encourage the client to sit on the toilet in case they do need to move their bowels. It is a great position to labor in, as it is an opportunity to be upright with the pelvis open. Mentally this can be a challenging time for the client as well. They may ask for pain medication during this time. Because there is a "code word" in place (from your discussion during the birth planning), you will work diligently and assertively to get the client over this hurdle. In a hospital birth setting, a vaginal exam will indicate full dilation (10cm) and will be done prior to the provider encouraging the pushing phase to begin. The provider will want to be certain that transitional labor is complete as pushing against a cervix that is not complete can cause irreversible swelling.

Second Stage - Pushing

Once it is determined that the cervix is completely dilated, clients giving birth in hospitals are given the "green light" to start pushing. For a client who is giving birth for the first time, the pushing stage can take 30 minutes to 3 hours. Hearing a team of doctors and nurses encouraging the client to push for a length of time, without the client seeing any progress, can cause them to feel defeated. During this time, the client has options and as their doula you can encourage them to express their preferences.

- **Coached pushing** is when the cervix is determined to be fully dilated and the provider or nurse (or both) coach the client to take a deep breath, hold it, and push for as long and as hard as they are able. They will be coached to do this 2-3 times during each contraction and encouraged to rest in between.
- **Passive descent** is when a client is not coached to push when they are determined to be fully dilated, but rather to continue to "labor the baby down," allowing the contractions to move the baby lower into the birth canal. In this scenario, the client relies on their own

intuition and the sensations their body is feeling in order to birth the baby. Their body tells them when to push and when to rest, and they trust their instincts.
- For some clients a **combination of both** of these techniques for the pushing stage can be incredibly valuable. A client may feel the need to have "some" coaching early on in the pushing phase but, once they have an understanding of "how" to push, they may prefer to follow their instincts. As the doula, your awareness of this will prompt you to help your client find what is best for them.

Laboring Down With an Epidural

In 2019 ACOG issued updated recommendations for their committee opinion titled, "Approaches to Limit Intervention During Labor and Birth." One of the two updated opinions focuses on new data for laboring down when epidural anesthesia is used.

The new recommendation states that: "Delayed pushing has not been shown to significantly improve the likelihood of vaginal birth and risks of delayed pushing, including infection, hemorrhage, and neonatal acidemia should be shared with nulliparous women receiving neuraxial analgesia who consider such an approach."
(Source: Approaches to Limit Intervention During Labor and Birth; Number 766 | February 2019)

In 2018, a multicenter randomized, controlled trial of over 2,400 nulliparous birthing individuals receiving epidural analgesia, assigned participants to start pushing at the beginning of the second stage of labor or to wait to begin pushing for 60 minutes unless the birthing person felt the urge to push, or health care provider recommended that pushing begin sooner. The trial was stopped early because of concern for excess complications in the delayed pushing group.
(Source: Effect of immediate vs delayed pushing on rates of spontaneous vaginal delivery among nulliparous women receiving neuraxial analgesia: a randomized clinical trial . JAMA 2018 ; 320 : 1444 – 54)

Individuals in the delayed pushing group saw increased rates of chorioamnionitis, postpartum hemorrhage, and more infants experienced acidemia.

Third Stage - The Placenta

Following the birth of the baby, the client will next have to deliver the placenta. This stage normally takes ~6 to 30 minutes. A physiological third stage refers to the "natural" delivery of the placenta without any interventions. The cord is given time to stop pulsing before being cut, no medications are administered, and the client pushes out the placenta with no assistance.

A managed third stage involves the administration of oxytocin either by intramuscular injection or via IV. Delivery of the placenta is achieved through the means of controlled cord traction and massage of the fundus, or top of the uterus, after the delivery of the placenta.

The "Golden Hour," the hour of time immediately following the delivery of the baby, also typically begins during this stage of labor. During the Golden Hour, the following things normally occur (unless baby requires immediate medical attention):

- Immediate, uninterrupted skin-to-skin contact between the baby and client
- Physical examinations of newborn conducted while on client's chest
- Weighing/measuring/testing delayed until after first feeding

Delayed Umbilical Cord Clamping

Current recommendations for delayed cord clamping from ACOG and endorsed by the American College of Nurse Midwives as of 2023 indicates:

> "Term and preterm infants appear to derive benefit from delayed umbilical cord clamping; therefore, delayed umbilical cord clamping for at least 30–60 seconds is recommended in term and preterm infants except when immediate umbilical cord clamping is necessary because of neonatal or maternal indications. In term infants, delayed umbilical cord clamping increases hemoglobin levels at birth and improves iron stores in the first several months of life, which may have a favorable effect on developmental outcomes."
> (Source: Delayed Umbilical Cord Clamping After Birth | Committee Opinion | Number 814 December 2020 | Reaffirmed 2023)

This committed opinion confirms that there are significant benefits to delayed cord clamping in term and preterm infants. The benefits for term infants are outlined in the citation above. The benefits for preterm infants are improved transitional circulation, improved red blood cell volume, less need for blood transfusion, and lower rates of necrotizing enterocolitis and intraventricular hemorrhage.

While there is a small increase in the rates of jaundice that may require phototherapy in term infants, this does not mean that delayed cord clamping should be avoided. Instead, ACOG recommends that birth facilities should ensure that mechanisms are in place to monitor and treat neonatal jaundice.

Laboring at Home: When You Will, When You Won't

As a doula, it is acceptable to labor at home with a client when the client is at least 37 weeks pregnant and:

- The client's bag of waters is intact
- The client's bag of waters is not intact BUT the fluid is clear and they are negative for Group B Strep
- Contractions are inconsistent
- Contractions are more than 4-5 minutes apart

It is not acceptable to labor at home with a client when the client is less than 37 weeks, and:

- The client has not contacted their medical provider
- The client's bag of waters is broken and there are signs of meconium (baby's first bowel movement) OR they are positive for Group B Strep
- Contractions are closer than 5 minutes apart, lasting a minute for at least an hour, and they are taking your client's breath away
- You OR your client are no longer comfortable laboring at home

Induction of Labor

There are many ways that labor can begin, however, they are not all spontaneous. For some of your clients, an induction of labor may be necessary or suggested. In order for you to be a well-rounded and supportive doula, it is essential that you understand why an induction of labor may be the chosen plan for your client and what decisions may accompany it along the way. Keep in mind that there are both natural methods and medical methods that are used to try to initiate labor.

When it comes to induction of labor there are two reasons that induction will be the chosen course of action.

- The health of the pregnant person or the baby dictates that the benefit of continuing the pregnancy does not outweigh the risk of induction.
- The patient chooses an elective induction of labor for non-medical reasons.

When a client makes the decision to accept an induction of labor, the doula's role is to support their decision. Helping them formulate questions to ask their provider can be beneficial to them as they work to gain a clear understanding of what they can expect. You can also have resources at hand to provide clients as they navigate these decisions.

When relaying information to a client, use your **B.R.A.I.N.**

- Benefits
- Risks
- Alternatives
- Instincts
- Nothing

This is a great way to present the facts. It will also enable you to ask thought provoking questions that will allow and encourage your client to make the best choices for themselves and their family.

Bishop Score

The Bishop Score is an assessment of the cervix prior to labor. It is used to determine the degree to which the cervix is "ready" for labor and whether or not an induction is likely to be successful.

During a vaginal exam a score is given in 5 categories and that score is totaled.

	SCORE			
	0	1	2	3
Position	Posterior	Midline	Anterior	-
Consistency	Firm	Medium	Soft	-
Dilation	Closed	1-2CM	3-4CM	5-6CM
Effacement	0-30%	40-50%	60-70%	80%+
Station	-3	-2	-1/0	+1/+2

- The highest possible score is 13.
- A score of 5 or less suggests that labor is unlikely to start without induction soon.
- A score of 9 or more indicates that labor will likely commence spontaneously.
- A low Bishop score often indicates that induction is unlikely to be successful.
- Some sources indicate that only a score of 8 or greater is reliably predictive of a successful induction.

Encourage your client to ask their provider about their Bishop Score in reference to induction. They will have a better understanding of the likelihood of success with this knowledge and can more easily decide if they feel ready for induction.

Notes:

Interventions & Medications

Stripping/Sweeping Membranes - The provider inserts a gloved finger into the vagina and through the cervical opening. They then use a sweeping motion to separate the amniotic membranes from the inside of the cervix. This intervention triggers the release of the hormone prostaglandin. Prostaglandin is responsible for causing the cervix to soften and ripen and also facilitate contractions of the uterus.

B - _____
R - _____
A - _____
I - _____
N - _____

Balloon Catheter - Foley or Cook - Depending on the provider and facility a Foley or Cook catheter may be used. The Foley catheter has one inflatable balloon on the end, while the Cook catheter has two. The catheter is passed into the vagina and through the cervix, where the first (or only) balloon is inflated with air or sterile water. The Cook catheter's second balloon is inflated on the outside of the cervix, essentially pressing on the cervix from both the inside and the outside. The pressure from the balloon(s) causes the cervix to dilate and efface. The goal is to increase the Bishop score in order to increase the likelihood of a successful induction.

B - _____
R - _____
A - _____
I - _____
N - _____

Cervidil - Cervidil (dinoprostone) is the only FDA approved vaginal insert for cervical ripening. Dinoprostone is a synthetic prostaglandin that aids in the ripening (softening) of the cervix in preparation for induction of labor. The medication is delivered via a vaginal insert that looks much like a shoestring with a rectangle of medication at one end. This rectangle is placed in the vagina, next to the cervix, to deliver the medication directly to the cervix. The remaining end of the string is used to remove the insert after 12 hours.

B - _____
R - _____
A - _____
I - _____
N - _____

Cytotec - Cytotec, or misoprostol, was once a hotly contested medication used to ripen the cervix in preparation for induction of labor. However, over 45 studies have shown that Cytotec is more effective than prostaglandin E2 (PE2) and oxytocin in facilitating vaginal delivery within 24 hours. It does not significantly increase adverse outcomes for birthing individuals or their babies as compared to PE2 or oxytocin. Cytotec is given via an oral slurry (drink) or via a tablet inserted vaginally.

B - _____
R - _____
A - _____
I - _____
N - _____

IV Catheter or Saline Lock - In many hospitals, it is standard procedure to administer an IV upon admission to labor & delivery. The IV catheter is a small, thin flexible catheter that is threaded into a vein that allows the medical staff to provide IV hydration and medications during the course of the labor, delivery, and recovery period. In some hospitals or birth centers, the IV catheter can be placed and capped off to allow freedom of movement and access to a shower or bath.

B - _____
R - _____
A - _____
I - _____
N - _____

Pitocin - Pitocin is a synthetic version of the hormone oxytocin. It causes contractions of the smooth muscle of the uterus and is used to induce or augment labor or to prevent or treat postpartum hemorrhage. When used to induce or augment labor it is given via IV and is delivered in metered doses.

B - _____
R - _____
A - _____
I - _____
N - _____

A.R.O.M - AROM is an acronym for the artificial rupturing of the amniotic sac, also known as amniotomy. Performed by a medical care provider using a specialized tool known as an amnihook or amnicot, or with the provider's fingers. The provider creates an opening in the bag of waters or amniotic sac to allow the fluid to be released. Releasing the fluid helps to apply the baby's head to the cervix and releases hormones that can aid in the facilitation of contractions. This procedure may be performed as part of an induction of labor, to attempt to augment or speed up labor, or to allow for internal monitoring via fetal scalp electrode or intrauterine pressure catheter.

B - _____
R - _____
A - _____
I - _____
N - _____

Rupture of Membranes

During pregnancy, the baby is surrounded by a fluid-filled, membranous sac called the amniotic sac. For some (less than 15%), the first sign of labor is when the amniotic membranes rupture, also known as "water breaking" or spontaneous rupture of membranes (SROM). When this happens and is not followed by contractions for more than one hour, it is referred to as a premature rupture of membranes (PROM). For others, it happens much later in the process, and, for some, the amniotic sac is ruptured artificially by the medical provider (AROM).

"I was a week late with my first baby and was convinced that my baby was NEVER COMING! They never said it was an estimated due date, they always said DUE DATE and when that date came and went and I didn't feel any different, I was pissed! No, literally! LOL!

I woke up one morning and went to the bathroom to pee. I got back into bed and a few moments later, more pee came out. I went back to the bathroom to pee again and clean myself up, I got back into bed and it happened again. I did this two more times before I got up, showered, and went to my OB appointment. It turned out my water had broken!"

For some clients, their water breaking is the first sign of labor. But for most, that is simply not the case. Sitcoms and comedians have mocked this part of labor and birth causing people to believe that birth begins when your water breaks. It seems to be the "funniest" way to say a person is in labor and everyone should panic!

Here is what your client should know:

- Only 10-15% of people begin labor with their water breaking.
- It is not always easy to tell if the water has broken; sometimes it is only a trickle and sometimes a "pop" is felt, followed by a big gush.
- The client should be prepared to describe any noticeable odor or color.

These are things that their provider will want to know: Color, Odor, Amount, Time (C.O.A.T.)

Color - Fluid should be clear. Yellow or greenish brown color would indicate that the baby has had a bowel movement in utero (meconium).
Odor - A mild or slightly musky smell is normal, but a strong odor may indicate infection.
Amount - Note whether it is a trickle or a gush. If the client is unsure if the water has broken, they should go to the bathroom, urinate, and then lie down on their side for 10-15 minutes and then stand up. If water has pooled in the vagina and it comes out when they stand up, it would be a strong indication that the water has broken.
Time - There are increased risks of infection as time passes once the water breaks. The provider may want to induce labor if contractions do not start on their own within a set period of time.

Additional Tips

- If the water breaks and the client is positive for Group B Strep, the provider will want them to come to the hospital right away so that they can administer antibiotics.
- If the water breaks and the client is not having contractions and is negative for Group B Strep, they might consider activities to try to

bring on the contractions. Walking can be helpful during this time
- Sometimes a provider will break the water to "help move labor along." A client always has a choice in this and has the right to have a conversation about this prior to it happening.
- Often the water will break on its own at some point during labor. If this happens, the nurse should be notified so that they can note the color, odor, amount, and time.
- For a small handful of clients (fewer than 1 in 80,000), their babies are "born in the caul." This is how we refer to babies born in the amniotic sac. The sac balloons out at birth with the amniotic fluid and child remaining in the unbroken membrane.

Braxton-Hicks Contractions

Braxton-Hicks contractions are sporadic uterine contractions. They generally begin about 6 weeks into pregnancy but most pregnant people do not feel them until the second trimester of pregnancy.

About Braxton-Hicks contractions:

- The uterine muscles tighten for 15-60 seconds.
- They usually feel like a mild tightening of the belly.
- Days or weeks before labor they may become rhythmic, close together, painful, or annoying.
- They do not consistently grow longer, stronger, and closer together
- Dehydration is often the cause.
- Changing activities or positions can help.
- Try using relaxation techniques, such as deep breathing, to help cope with the discomfort.

When your client calls their midwife or obstetrician, they will be asked how far apart the contractions are, how long they are lasting, and how intense they are.

If the client is timing them incorrectly, they could be asked to come into the hospital sooner than they would like.

Timing Contractions

When timing contractions:

Use a stopwatch that calculates seconds or an app specific to timing contractions.

The length of a contraction is measured from the time it begins to the time it ends. The time between contractions is measured from the time a contraction begins, to the time the next one begins.

Timing Contractions

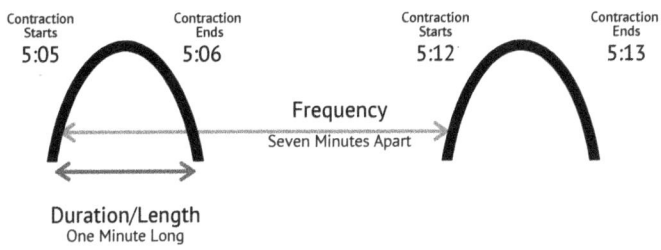

When to call the doctor or midwife:

If the client has not reached 37 weeks and any of the following occur:

- Contractions are more frequent and painful
- Menstrual-like cramping
- Vaginal bleeding
- Vaginal discharge or a change in the type of discharge
- Pressure in the pelvic area
- Low back pain that is dull or rhythmic

Contractions that prompt the client to go to the hospital are referred to as 5-1-1. This means that the contractions are 5 minutes apart, lasting for 1 minute, and that this has been the pattern for at least 1 hour.

Consider how well the client is managing the labor physically and emotionally. If the contractions are 5-1-1 and the client is chatting and joking, they are likely not in active labor just yet. If the contractions are 5-1-1 and the client must use all of their focus and breath to manage through them, they are likely in active labor.

As you become more and more experienced as a doula these signs will become more and more clear to you.

Shifting Gears

It's happening. Right now. This second. Oooh, it just happened again. You were at work or asleep or making breakfast or arguing with your teenager about procrastinating on an assignment and, unto a family, a child was born.

For that family the Earth stood still. Everything stopped for them and nothing else mattered. Phones began to ring shortly after the child was born and those people were included in the celebration.

The people unaffected had no idea of this special "secret" and their lives continued. They continued sleeping, making breakfast, working, arguing.

But what about the people in between? The birth workers? Those people are both affected AND unaffected. Let me explain.

I am the doula. It is not my birth. It is not my baby. It is not my experience. I do not hold the details of my client's birth with me when I leave. I simply have been given the honor of standing by their side and serving them and their partner on their path to family. I am both present and scarce at the same time and I take no ownership over their experience.

As I get into my car and begin to drive to a client in labor, often I get a signal from the world to shift gears. It can be the smell in the air, a star filled night, or a gorgeous sunset that I take in on my way to the birth. I find myself acutely aware that the world is whispering to me: shift gears, a child is about to be born.

These signals act as a reminder for me. They remind me to open. To open myself to the needs and desires of others. To open myself up and allow the strength and wisdom of the hundreds and hundreds of people I have served in birth before this to flow through me and fill the birth space with their strength and wisdom.

Often, moments after my client gives birth, they look at me gratefully and tenderly and say something like, "I couldn't have done it without you," but I know it is not true. They are simply saying thank you to the people I have served before them. I quietly acknowledge the spirit of those people and I remind my client that THEY did all of the work!

Things settle down and soon after a look comes over the eyes of my clients that they are ready to bond as a family. I take one last photo for them, wish their baby a Happy Birthday, dim the lights, and head out the door. I say goodbye to the nurses, doctors, cleaning folks, and security guard on my way out to my car and my life continues.

It's 9:00am. I stop at the grocery store for a gallon of milk and the cashier smiles at me and says, "How's your morning going?" I chuckle to myself and say, "Pretty good, how's yours?"

Authored by: Randy Patterson - ProDoula CEO

Notes:

Sharing the Benefits of Doula Support

Beginning your new career as a doula is undoubtedly exciting, but it can also feel a little daunting. Afterall, you will need to find clients in order to begin your work in this field. Newer doulas can sometimes feel lost or directionless when it comes to doing this. The following tips are meant to ease your fears and prepare you to confidently share the benefits of doula support with everyone, future clients included.

Elevator Speech

An "elevator speech" is a short summary used to quickly and simply define a person, product, service, or organization and its promise of value to be delivered. The name reflects the idea that it should be possible to deliver the summary in the time span of an elevator ride or approximately thirty seconds to two minutes.

Exercise

When writing your elevator speech, start with a list of what you want to include:

About YOU

- Your name and what you do
    - "Hi, I'm Sally White. I'm a doula."

About what you offer

- Explain the service that you offer
- Describe it
    - "Doulas serve families through pregnancy, birth, and the postpartum period...."
- Be prepared to alter this based on your listener's level of understanding of what a doula is

Creat the value

- Describe the benefits of doula support
- Make it relative to you
    - "Having a doula attend your birth can decrease your risk of a cesarean birth and improve overall satisfaction...."

- "As your doula, I would…."

Validate it

- How long have you been a doula
- Why did you become a doula
- The organization you certified with and why
    - "I have been a doula for two years. I felt called to this work during my pregnancy when I learned the benefits of a doula and then I sought out the education. I chose ProDoula because…."

Call to action

- Offer your business card and ask if you can follow up with them
- "I would love to connect with you again to discuss this further. Would you be interested in that?"

Doula Consultations

A consultation is an opportunity for you and a potential client to determine your compatibility. Sometimes referred to as an interview, these consults allow you to share your expertise and enable the prospective client to imagine themselves giving birth with your support.

Each consult will be unique to the family that has invited you in. In some cases, expectant parents will have a list of questions like the ones below and, in other cases, you will lead them through the process of getting to know you.

Consultations should include these four steps.

1. Getting to Know You - This should be casual and relaxed. It is an opportunity to get to know a bit about each other and create a positive energy for the remainder of the visit together.
2. Learning Birth Philosophies - An exploration of the potential client's hopes and wishes for their birth.
3. Painting a Picture - An explanation of your support and how it can assist them in achieving their goals.
4. Closing the Sale - An invitation for them to engage your services.

Use these questions and their answers as a guide for preparing for your consultations.

- Will you answer my questions without bias?
- Will you judge me if I make different decisions than you would?
- Will you respect the relationship my partner and I have, even with all of its imperfections?
- Are you equipped with a variety of strategies for supporting all types of labor and birth?
- Are you competent and capable?
- Are you accountable and available?
- Do you have a back-up system in place in the event that you are unavailable?
- Do you have a legal contract in place?
- Did you take a hands-on, in-person doula training?
- Are you supported by a reputable training organization with a grievance policy in place?

During the consultation, open a discussion about the client taking a childbirth education class. Let them know that you will schedule your prenatal visit with them for a mutually convenient time shortly after they do so and ask if they have signed up for one. This is an excellent opportunity to encourage them to take their CBE class with you if you offer this service. Let them know that a good childbirth education class will present all of their options for labor and birth. Taking this class before the prenatal meeting will prepare them to discuss their birth preferences with you.

Teaching childbirth classes further positions you as an expert in the field. If you are not already a Childbirth Educator, consider adding this certification to your resume. This ProDoula Labor Doula Training serves as the prerequisite needed to register for ProDoula's Childbirth Educator Training.

Prenatal Schedule for Healthy Pregnancies

As a doula it is important to have knowledge regarding your clients medical care.

While each pregnancy is unique and the exact schedule of visits may vary slightly from individual to individual, the following is an overview of prenatal visits and prenatal testing in the United States.

According to the National Institutes of Health, prenatal visits typically occur:

- Before the 28th week - Every four weeks
- Weeks 28-36 - Every two weeks
- Week 36 through birth - Every week
    (Source: https://www.nichd.nih.gov/health/topics/preconceptioncare/conditioninfo/prenatal-visits)

The first prenatal visit may happen around the 8th week of pregnancy unless there is a history of medical problems, miscarriage, spotting or bleeding.

Routine Prenatal Visit - Approximate Gestation	
First Prenatal Visit - 8-10 weeks	• Review of medical history • Lab work - Screening for STIs and immunity to certain diseases such as rubella, determine RH factor • Possible ultrasound for dating of pregnancy • Physical Exam • Weight • Blood pressure
12 Weeks	• Review of previous lab work • Weight and blood pressure • Urine screening - depending on provider • First trimester genetic screening • Check fetal heart tones
16 Weeks	• Weight, blood pressure • Measure fundal height • Check fetal heart tones • Additional screening for genetic defects offered
20 Weeks	• Weight, blood pressure • Measure fundal height • Check fetal heart tones • Anatomy scan
24 Weeks	• Weight, blood pressure • Measure fundal height • Check fetal heart tones
28 Weeks	• Weight, blood pressure • Measure fundal height • Check fetal heart tones • Screen for gestational diabetes • If Rh negative, first Rhogam shot given
30 Weeks	• Weight, blood pressure • Measure fundal height • Check fetal heart tones • Review gestational diabetes screening results

32 Weeks	• Weight, blood pressure • Measure fundal height • Check fetal heart tones
34 Weeks	• Weight, blood pressure • Measure fundal height • Check fetal heart tones
36 Weeks	• Weight, blood pressure • Measure fundal height • Check fetal heart tones • Group B Strep test • Cervical check (with some providers)
37 Weeks - Birth	• Weight, blood pressure • Measure fundal height • Check fetal heart tones • Cervical check • Possible discussion of induction of labor or scheduling of a cesarean depending on the individual's circumstances

Writing a Birth Plan

Many clients look forward to writing a "birth plan." They view it as an opportunity to organize their thoughts and finalize their decisions regarding their birth preferences.

However, nothing is final in birth and sometimes, based on circumstances, the plan must change. Consider the birth plan discussion an opportunity for you to REALLY get to know your client.

When helping a client navigate through the process of exploring their birth preferences it is important to keep DISC in mind. Understanding the personality style of the client will help you navigate the process they will most likely be attuned to when it comes to formulating decisions surrounding their preferences.

> **D** personalities typically "go with their gut." They have a natural tendency toward decisiveness.
> **I** personalities value social acceptance when it comes to decision making. They often ask what others have or would do.
> **S** personalities can really struggle with decision making and can have a tendency to avoid it. The fear of the unknown can be paralyzing for them.
> **C** personalities focus on the research and evidence when making decisions. The process can be lengthy but the decision reached is a confident one.

When organizing a birth plan with a client, help them write a list of their wishes rather than a rigid plan. Be sure to advise them as to whether or not their wishes fall within the routine protocols of the birth location they have chosen. If not, encourage the client to contact their provider and hospital administrator to discuss their wishes to implement a choice that falls outside of protocol.

Keep the list simple and avoid asking for things that are routinely typical in the facility of choice. Birth plan worksheets that are easily accessible online can be overly detail-oriented and can make the medical staff feel as if they are being micromanaged. This can be off-putting and may lead to unnecessary discord between the medical provider and the client.

Walk Through the Process

Walk your clients through the birth process starting with the onset of labor and ending with the initial decisions parents of a newborn must make. Remember, it doesn't all need to be part of the written plan, but it is important to make sure you understand your client's wishes.

Discuss Each Possibility of the Onset of Labor

Spontaneous Labor

Spontaneous labor or Spontaneous Vaginal Delivery (SVD) occurs when a pregnant person goes into labor without the use of medications or techniques to induce labor. They deliver their baby in the "normal" manner without forceps, vacuum extraction, or cesarean birth.

This is the most common type of delivery and the one by which all other modes of delivery are compared.

Spontaneous labor can begin in a number of ways:

- Mild contractions typically sporadic in nature and lasting 15-30 seconds. These contractions are best described as similar to menstrual cramps or an aching sensation in the front or low back.
- A spontaneous rupture of membranes (breaking of water) with contractions following and increasing gradually in length and strength.
- A spontaneous rupture of membranes (breaking of water) without being accompanied by contractions.
- The mucus plug, which protects the uterus from bacteria, may be passed during the onset of labor.

There are several things that can influence the decision not to have a spontaneous vaginal delivery. These include complete placenta previa (when the placenta forms over the cervix and a vaginal delivery can cause severe hemorrhaging). Or if the client has the herpes virus with active lesions or they have untreated HIV, as both can be passed to the baby through a vaginal birth. Or if the client or baby has another medical need or reason for induction or cesarean birth.

Prodromal Labor

Prodromal labor is an early phase of labor that does not progress in a "normal pattern." Contractions do not increase in intensity and cervical dilation is minimal. However, this is part of labor for some clients and can be physically and emotionally very difficult. Many refer to this as "false labor," which can be received negatively by the person experiencing it. Keeping your client positive and encouraging rest will be crucial to their birth experience.

- Physically
    - Contractions are uncomfortable
    - The client is unable to sleep well
    - The client becomes exhausted before difficult labor begins
- Emotionally
    - Initially the client is excited that labor is beginning
    - The client mentally prepares themself to give birth and is disappointed that labor is not increasing in intensity
    - The client may begin to doubt their ability to continue
    - The client may doubt their body's ability to birth "normally"
    - The client may begin to re-think their birth wishes

Therapeutic rest (utilizing medication in the hospital for the purpose of forced rest) for an exhausted client experiencing prodromal labor over several days may not be part of their original birth wishes, but may be exactly what they need to completely relax their body for a couple of hours. There is a good chance they may wake in a solid pattern of labor.

Precipitous Labor

This refers to a delivery which results after an unusually rapid labor (less than three hours) and culminates in the rapid, spontaneous birth of the infant. A birth of this nature can be very overwhelming to your client and can have physical and emotional side effects.

- Physical
    - Very strong labor without warning
    - The client may be less prepared for the pain
    - Delivering the baby quickly can cause more trauma at the perineum (tearing)

- Emotional

- The client may be extremely overwhelmed
- The client may doubt themselves in relation to actually being in labor due to the assumption that labor is expected to be more time consuming
- The client may doubt their ability to cope with the labor
- The client may feel very afraid
- May create additional fear regarding future births

Ask their thoughts, fears, concerns, and preferences in relation to each scenario. Remind them to stay in close contact with you as they begin to experience any of the following things:

- Prodromal labor
- Precipitous labor
- Onset of mild contractions
- Spontaneous rupture of membranes with contractions
- Spontaneous rupture of membranes without contractions
- Induction
    - Cytotec
    - Cervidil
    - Balloon Catheter
    - Pitocin
    - AROM

Next, discuss when you will join them. Explain that you will be talking periodically throughout the early stage of labor. When they decide that they would like you to be present, that is when the face-to-face labor support will begin. You will be joining them in their home or in the hospital, based on their preference. Discuss each possibility of this stage and ask their thoughts, fears, concerns, and preferences in relation to each scenario.

- Who will attend the birth?
- Discuss options for how you will all get to the hospital from their house
- Outline what will happen upon arrival at the hospital:
    - Change into a gown
    - Monitoring of baby and contractions for a period of time
    - Have a cervical exam
    - Have blood drawn
    - Have an IV started (when this is routine protocol)
    - Answer questions about health history
    - Present birth plan

Code Word

Have a heart-to-heart discussion about the client's wishes in relation to pain management. Suggest a "code word" to use in a situation where they have changed their mind and do not want to be coached beyond what they are comfortable with. Remind the client that they are in charge and this is their experience. You are there to support them and if the plan changes, you want to know so that you can support the "new plan." Discuss medications used for pain management. Explore each possibility of these options and ask the client's thoughts, fears, concerns, and preferences in relation to each scenario.

- Massage
- Breathing techniques
- Position changes
- Vocalization
- Hypnotherapy
- Bath/Shower
- Epidural
- Narcotics
  - DEMEROL (meperidine)
  - Fentanyl
  - STADOL (butorphanol tartrate)

Discuss possible interventions with your client. Ask about their thoughts, fears, concerns, and preferences in relation to each scenario.

- Vaginal exams
- Artificial rupture of membranes (AROM)
- Pitocin
- Monitoring (constant/intermittent) (external/internal)
- Catheter for urination
- IV fluids
- Vacuum extraction
- Forceps delivery

Describe the pushing phase to your clients. Explain the difference between passive descent and coached pushing. Explain to your client that they do not have to decide now what will serve them best in labor, but having a sense of this ahead of time will be helpful.

- Coached pushing

- Passive descent
- Positions for pushing

Paint a picture of what the actual delivery might look like. Ask what the partner sees as their role during this part and what their comfort level is in participation. (Are they an "up north" kind of person or a "get right in there" kind of person?) Discuss each possible scenario and ask their thoughts, fears, concerns, and preferences in relation to each scenario.

- Perineal massage
- Episiotomy
- Touching the baby's head while crowning
- Partner touching the baby's head
- Skin-to-skin (don't assume they want it immediately)
- Who speaks or doesn't speak during this time
- Who announces the sex of the baby
- Delayed cord clamping
- Cord blood banking
- Ask if partner or client would like to cut the cord
- Pictures of the actual delivery
- Anything else that they might like to see happen during this time

Next, explain to your client the process of waiting for the placenta to detach and the delivery of it. Discuss options in regard to the placenta after the birth.

- Disposing of the placenta as medical waste
- Lotus birth (only applies to home birth)
- Ingestion of the placenta
- Placenta encapsulation
- The placenta as fertilizer

Finally, address the various newborn practices and procedures. Discuss each procedure and common occurrence. Ask the client's thoughts, fears, concerns, and preferences in relation to each scenario.

- APGAR
- Breastfeeding
- Hepatitis B
- Vitamin K
- Erythromycin
- Weight/measurements

- Pacifiers/formula
- Rooming-in/nursery

Example #1 Sample Birth Plan Wish List:

(Partner's name) and I would like to thank our doctors, midwife, and the staff of (Name of hospital) for being so supportive of our choices thus far. We would like to express a few desires in this birth plan so that you have a good understanding of our wishes for the birth of our baby.

- We are hoping to have a natural, unmedicated birth. We are hoping to avoid an episiotomy.
- We are open to giving birth in the tub.
- We would like our doula to photograph our birth.
- We would like (Partner's name) to help guide the baby out, if it is appropriate at the time.
- We would like to delay cord clamping.
- We would like to take our placenta home with us.
- We would like to decline the Hep-B vaccine in the hospital.
- We would like to breastfeed exclusively.

Thank you again for your support and understanding of our wishes. These memories will last a lifetime for us.

Example #2

Birth Preferences for: (Client name) My partner and my doula will be present.

- I would like as much privacy as possible.
- I would like the lights to be dimmed.
- I would like to be reminded to empty my bladder hourly.
- I would like to remain as active as possible, finding the best positions for me and changing these as I wish.
- I would like to rest between contractions whenever possible.
- I would like monitoring of the baby to be kept to a minimum unless there is cause for concern.
- Please use a hand-held Doppler, as opposed to constant fetal monitoring.
- I would prefer to avoid all interventions unless a medical emergency precipitates them.

I would like information about any proposed medication prior to receiving it: the purpose, potential side effects on me or the baby, and the timing of said medication.

- I would like to use hypnosis, hydrotherapy, massage, and movement to manage the discomfort of my labor.
- I do not want anyone to offer me any pain medication during my labor or birth.
- I would like to stay in the tub as long as possible, including the birth if I feel so inclined.
- I would like to find an upright, comfortable position for pushing. Advice will be welcome.
- I would like to know when my baby is crowning. I would like firm advice and guidance at this time to guard against tearing.
- I do not wish to have an episiotomy unless medically vital or I agree to it.
- I would like to have skin-to-skin contact with my baby immediately and would like to discover the sex of my baby myself. Please do not announce this when my baby is born.
- Ideally, I would like my baby to come to the breast on their own when they are ready. I would like any help in positioning the baby that you can offer.
- I wish the cord to remain attached until it stops pulsating.
- My partner would like to cut the umbilical cord.
- If I have had a natural birth, I would like a physiological third stage.
- If a tear occurs, I want to be advised whether or not I require stitches. I will choose then whether or not I will want local pain relief.
- I wish to be stitched by an experienced doctor or midwife and not a student.

Support When Plans Change

A birth plan is a list of wishes or desires for one's birth journey and although it is important to have an open mind to some degree, many clients feel very connected to their wishes. This can cause great disappointment if their expectations are not met.

During the birth planning session, discussing whether or not the client trusts their provider can be valuable information. If they do not trust their provider, that may be something they should explore further.

Support them by reminding them that just because part of the plan changes does not mean the whole plan must change. Encourage them to make decisions that feel best for them and re-focus them on the parts of the plan that are what they wished for.

A client who feels as if their plan "failed" can put them at increased risk for postpartum depression or other mood and anxiety disorders. Birth trauma can also increase the risk of postpartum mood and anxiety disorders.

Some things that can cause birth trauma may include:

- Long labor
- Induction
- Failed pain relief
- Many interventions
- Not feeling "heard"
- Baby going to the NICU
- History of sexual abuse
- Unplanned/unwanted cesarean birth

Resource for a client struggling after cesarean birth
- ICAN (International Cesarean Awareness Network)

Placenta Encapsulation

Placenta encapsulation is a process in which the placenta is steamed, dehydrated, crushed into powder form, and placed into gel capsules for consumption.

There has not been a tremendous amount of research done on this topic, however, the anecdotal evidence that supports the benefits are undeniable.

Individuals who ingest their own placentas via encapsulation (and many other methods) are reporting increased milk production, increased energy levels, and a decrease in PMADs. This evidence is most useful in those who have had more than one pregnancy/birth. These individuals have shared that they experience a more positive postpartum period after ingesting their encapsulated placentas as opposed to when they did not.

Things to Caution Clients Of:

- The placenta is being prepared for ingestion. For that reason, it should be either prepared or frozen as soon as possible post-birth
- Different states/counties have varying rules and regulations for the preparation of "food" for the ingestion of others. Placentas do not currently fall explicitly into this category, however, we believe it to be best practice to act in accordance with such regulations.
- Different states/counties and hospitals have varying regulations on who may remove the placenta from the hospital and transport it. We believe it to be best practice for the client to transport the placenta back to their own home.
- Making arrangements before the birth of the baby can help the client be more prepared.
- Arriving at the hospital with the necessary "supplies" for proper storage and transportation: 2 gallon-sized Ziploc bags (to double bag the placenta), cooler/cooler bag to place the sealed placenta in, and ice from an ice machine to keep the placenta cold during transport.

Getting Comfortable With Touch

Let us start by remembering that the skin is our largest organ. It is extremely sensitive and responsive, which lends itself to comfort, healing, and attunement.

There have been numerous studies indicating the beneficial effect of touch on our perception of pain. **"Touch is important for survival itself. We are meant to be touched. It is part of our inherent genetic development."** - massage therapist Elliot Green of Silver Spring, MD, past president of the American Massage Therapy Association (AMTA).

Not everyone is comfortable with touch. In our society, we have moved away from people greeting each other with hugs and kisses and/or with any type of physical contact in work environments. It is important that you practice and incorporate touch into your daily activities so that you become comfortable with receiving and giving touch. As a result, you will become more confident when providing support through touch.

Touch with your client starts with a greeting between doula and client and grows from there.

Will you greet them with a handshake or a hug?

Touch During Labor

Many clients will find massage to be helpful during labor. When touch comes with insecurity, the recipient senses it. If you are nervous when touching another person, they will feel the same awkwardness about it that you do. It is imperative that you touch with confidence.

Massage provides relaxation. Applying pressure or counter-pressure helps relieve pain.

*During a contraction, the movement and stimulation of massage is distracting to the client. Massage during relaxation periods and apply counter-pressure during contractions.

Prepare to touch by:

- Washing your hands
- Asking the client for permission to touch them
- Asking if there are any parts of the body that they prefer not to be

touched
- Exuding confidence

Quick Tips

- Use the heel of your hand to apply pressure to the sacrum.
- Stroke around the lower back.
- Use your thumbs to massage the lower back, use a circular motion and work from the base of the spine down until you reach the buttocks.
- Initiate gentle and light conversation while passing positive energy to the client.
- Be relaxed and comfortable while touching.
- Don't let go. Always keep one hand on the client while switching hands or positions.
- Be deliberate with your breath and sounds.

Dr. Tiffany Field of the Touch Research Institute conducted several studies on the effects of massage in pregnancy and labor. She discovered that when laboring individuals were massaged during labor, their labor shortened on average by three hours and they were less likely to need pain medication.

(Source: Pregnancy & Labor Massage, Tiffany Field; Expert Rev Obstet Gynecol. 2010 Mar; 5(2): 177–181)

Notes:

Comfort Measures

Common comfort measures include, but are not limited to:

- Lighting
- Peaceful environment
- Quiet/privacy
- Music (to the client's preferences)
- Warm/cool, hot/cold
- Massage
- Hair brushing
- Talking
- Aromatherapy
- Candles (battery operated if in hospital)

Heat

- Tub or shower
- Rice sock
- Heating pad
- Warm compress held to the perineum
- Warm massage oil

Cold

- Ice pack
- Cold compress/washcloth
- Ice chips
- Fan/fanning
- Placing your hands in an ice bath prior to touch

Concerning the Mind

- Visualizations
- Bringing focus to the breath
- Hypnosis
- Affirmations
- Focal point

Vocalization

- Deep low tones; OOOOOH, OOOHM

Pressure

- Counter-pressure
- Double hip squeeze
- Knee pressure
- Head and base of neck pressure

Affirmations

Take a moment and begin developing your inner "doula voice." Create some verbal affirmations that feel authentic to you.

1.

2.

3.

4.

5.

6.

7.

8.

9.

10.

Partner Support

In many cases, if the client has a partner they are essential to their support. Your role as a doula includes supporting them, as well. A critical part of forming a connection as a doula is attuning to the partner and to the two of them as a couple.

When working with clients, doulas must not make assumptions about what the birthing person will want from their partner during labor. This is a conversation that should take place between you and the couple during the prenatal visit. Discuss how the partner can provide physical and emotional support and what that could look like. Have the birthing person reflect on the types of touch they find most comforting, as well as how they will best receive emotional encouragement from them. Encourage them to share these things with their partner.

During labor, you can model massage and comfort techniques that the partner or other support people can initiate and offer them reassurance and encouragement as well. Remind the partner to stay nourished and hydrated and let them know when an appropriate time to step out to use the bathroom, eat, or make a phone call arises. Remember the things you discussed with the couple during the prenatal and suggest some of them if the partner has forgotten to initiate those ideas themself.

It's also important for you, the doula, to be mindful of how things unfold in the moment. It's possible that the partner will find themselves unable to fulfill either the physical or emotional support role that the birthing person wanted from them. If the partner is overwhelmed or fearful, you may need to validate those feelings and encourage them to take a moment. You might have to step in and support the client in the way they need until their partner is able to rejoin them.

Or it's possible that in labor, the birthing person will not respond to the comfort measures they thought would work and can get frustrated if the partner persists in those. Some carefully worded questions between contractions - such as "Is what your partner doing working for you?" or "Would you like your partner to try a new technique?" - can help these two people reconnect in the throes of labor.

Labor Positions

Moving from position to position during labor is as important as the position itself. Imagine a client in labor moving from a standing position to a side lying position. They will likely have to sit first and then move one leg on to the bed, shimmy their bottom a bit, move the other leg on to the bed, shimmy a bit more, etc.

Now think about all of the activity their pelvis saw along the way. Opening and moving the pelvis during labor provides more space for their baby to make the necessary movements to be born. Encourage your client to exaggerate their movements when they are changing positions during labor.

The five basic positions for labor are as follows (we will experiment with creative variations of each position):

Upright/Standing (Taking advantage of gravity while using the partner, doula, or an object for support)

- Walking
- Slow dancing
- Lunging
- Bending at waist leaning on bed or other surface
- Hugging

Side Lying (Lying on side with knees and hips bent with a pillow or peanut ball between them)

- The bicycle position

Squatting (Wide open legs, coupled with gravity, make this an optimal position in labor)

- Partner squatting, supported squat, birth stool
- Squat/Birth bar

Sitting/Birth Ball (This position has moderate gravity advantages and may be useful while being monitored or in need of rest)

- Sitting on toilet
- Rear facing on toilet or chair
- Rocking chair for pelvic movement

- Sitting on birth ball
- Rocking side-to-side on birth ball
- The "throne position" in the hospital bed (back of bed all the way up, feet of bed all he way down)

Hands and Knees (With upper body on hands, over a birth ball or leaning over the top of the upright bed)

- On bed or floor
- Rocking the pelvis
- Cat/Cow
- Sitting on birth ball leaning on lowered bed

Laboring in Bed

Laboring on one's back (laying in bed) can be incredibly challenging. However, in many hospital settings a great deal of fetal monitoring is required and the nurse may imply that it should be done while in bed. Suggest that your client ask about sitting in a rocking chair or on a birth ball (exercise ball) while being monitored. This will likely be more comfortable and they will be utilizing gravity in the process. If the nurse insists that the client be in bed during this time, try some of the following comfort measures.

- Place a rolled up towel under the client's back for counterpressure
- Reach under the client and apply pressure with your hands/fists
- Stand at the end of the bed and have the client place their feet on your thighs; applying pressure against you during contractions can be both comforting and distracting
- Utilize touch and relaxation massage between contractions to enable the client to stay relaxed and feel supported through this difficult time

Pushing Positions

Pushing is done most effectively when the client feels an unbearable urge to push; when they almost can't stop themselves from pushing even when they try. In a home birth setting, a client is typically not even spoken to about pushing without this sensation. However, in a hospital birth setting, they will likely be more closely monitored. Once they have reached complete dilation, the care provider will usually encourage them to start pushing during contractions.

Early Pushing

During the early stages of pushing, clients that are encouraged to push before they feel the urge to do so can have a difficult time figuring out how to do it. Suggesting that the client sit on the toilet through some contractions and bear down during them can help stimulate them to connect with the idea that proper pushing is very similar to pushing to relieve the bowel.

Trying a variety of positions for pushing will not only help a client understand the most effective way to push, but it can help them find the most comfortable way as well.

Depending on the birth facility of choice, options available may include:

- Squatting
- Using a birth bar
- Sitting on a birth stool
- Hands and knees
- Side lying
- Standing
- Lunging
- Back lying

Historically, birthing people have been told to (or made to) lie on their backs and put their feet in stirrups when it is time to push. They are told to put their hands behind their thighs and pull back and open them wide. At the same time they are coached to bring their chin to their chest and bear down with all of their might.

Some clients choose to give birth at home, in a birth center, or in a hospital that offers more options so that they will have the opportunity to push in a position that best suits them at the moment.

Clients who are utilizing an epidural for pain relief are not permitted to leave the bed and may require additional physical support as they push.

Coached Pushing

Coached pushing refers to being guided or coached on how and when to push by the provider.

While the client is in this position and as a contraction builds, they are told to take a deep breath in, hold it, let it go, quickly take another deep breath in, hold it, bring their chin to their chest (as if to curl around their baby), pull back on their legs, and bear down with all of their might while the doctor or nurse counts to 10. They are told to release their breath, quickly take another one, hold it, and bear down again for a count to 10. Typically the provider will want the client to do this 3 times for each contraction.

The provider may use their fingers to apply pressure in the vagina to help direct the client on where to focus their pushing. This may be more commonly seen in clients who have had an epidural.

Passive Descent

This involves the client allowing their body to "labor the baby down" by continuing to focus on managing contractions and relaxation. The pushing phase does not begin until the client feels the unbearable urge to push and cannot resist it. Once the client feels this sensation, they are supported as they push through each contraction.

Notes:

Push your baby out!

Push?! Now? How? Like this? Am I doing it? Stop? UGH! Does this sound familiar? It doesn't have to.

In fact, birth will actually happen even if no one screams anything at you while you do it!

Knowing that we are fully dilated isn't always the best news of the day. When giving birth in a hospital, we are often given the impression that complete dilation means we made it, we're finished laboring. We are ready to push. Our cervix is completely out of the way and now we can simply push our baby out.

However, anyone who pushed for 2, 3, or 4+ hours would disagree with this. The truth is, 10cm is part of the process. It's an important part of the process BUT it is just one part.

Continuing to labor or as they say, "breathing the baby down," will decrease your pushing time dramatically. Think about it - if you poop every morning after drinking a cup of coffee and Tuesday morning you wake up and drink a cup of coffee but don't feel like you have to poop, you can sit on the toilet and push all day. If you don't feel like you have to poop, you're right!

No one screaming, "Push! You drank the coffee, you're ready! Push!" is going to get you to push a poop out! As we know, the best way to poop is to wait until you feel the "I have to poop" sensation, go somewhere private (preferably the bathroom), drop your pants, and poop.

The same can be said for pushing a baby out of your vagina. You are not required to push just because you are 10cm dilated. Let your body and your baby work together. Don't hold yourself accountable to your cervical dilation and don't let anyone else hold you accountable to it. If your doctor wants to know what your cervix is doing and you don't, you have a choice. You can say, "No thank you, I prefer not to have an exam." You can say, "I don't mind having an exam, but I don't want to know your findings and I don't want your findings to impact my process." You can say, "I'd love an exam; I can't wait to hear what you find!" You can say anything YOU want! It's your cervix and your vagina that's being examined.

After attending more than 1,000 births, I am certain that those who push when their bodies tell them to, have a much easier time giving birth than those who are instructed to push based on the findings of a cervical exam.

There are, of course, exceptions to every rule, but when a person's body is urging them to push and they do what their body indicates, they report feeling more in control, safer, and more comfortable in the birthing process.

Authored by: Randy Patterson - ProDoula CEO

Fear During Pushing

The fear of "pooping on the table" can inhibit some clients from pushing with their full potential. Remind your client that if there is stool in the lower bowel when they push, it will likely come out. Let them know that it is normal and that it is a great indication that they are pushing adequately.

What's your "thing?"

We all have a "thing." For some it's the IV and for others it's being seen naked.

For me, it was the poop thing…. I was totally freaked out by the idea that while pushing my baby out of my vagina an unwelcome piece of digested food might find its way out as well. I was absolutely fixated on this and I seriously considered asking my doctor for a cesarean birth to avoid it.

I was 25 years old. It was my first pregnancy and at that time in my life I suppose I cared what people thought about me.

I made my partner promise me that if poop came out of my butt, as long as I lived on the Earth, they would never tell me! To this day, if I say, "Did I poop when I pushed?" The answer is always the same, "No, you didn't." What I now know as a veteran doula with a tremendous amount of experience is that MOST of us poop when we push. If there is stool in the lower bowel and you bear down with incredible force, it will come out. No biggie, right? Well, sometimes it's a biggie….

Labor is often about letting go of the mind and embracing the body. I don't mean separating the two because I believe they are one. It's like focusing on your right hand while you're drawing and letting go of your left. Your left hand is still part of your body, but your focus is on the right. Only our mind would prevent us from bearing down to birth our baby from fear of pooping. Our body would never consider trying to shut down that process.

Now, here's the tricky part: Our mind keeps us safe! It strategically protects us from our fears. If we fear being judged or being vulnerable or being mocked, if poop freaks us out, or if we have created a bizarre visual in our mind of lying in a white-sheeted bed with fluorescent lighting overhead and a giant poop *coming out of our bodies, the mind will freeze the body.*

So, who will you invite into that room? What will the conversation be with that person or people leading up to your birth? Are they people that you can confidently and safely separate your mind and body in front of? Will you be able to allow your body to function the way it knows how to, the way it was designed to, the way it is intended to, in front of these people?

Who will you completely "let go" in front of?

I must tell you, I pride myself on being the kind of person that people can poop in front of during birth.

Authored by: Randy Patterson, ProDoula CEO

Further Interventions/Medications

Previously, this manual discussed interventions and medications that are commonly used during an induction of labor. But you will also encounter interventions and medications throughout all stages of labor. Some will be needed to monitor how the baby is tolerating labor, while others will be used to augment labor if it has stalled or provide comfort to the birthing person. Below, we will discuss each of these interventions and medications, along with their benefits, risks, and alternatives.

Fetal Monitoring - Doppler - During labor, the provider will want to monitor the fetal heart tones in response to contractions. This can be achieved by external monitoring of the fetal heart tones via doppler. The provider may use a handheld doppler to listen to the baby's heart tones through, and just after, a contraction. Or two belts secured to the client's belly may be used. One belt monitors the fetal heartbeat via doppler, and the other measures the frequency and duration of the contractions.

B - _____
R - _____
A - _____
I - _____
N - _____

Fetal Scalp Electrode - Internal Fetal Monitoring - Internal fetal monitoring is facilitated via a thin electrode attached most commonly to the fetal scalp. This thin electrode is threaded through the vagina and passed through the cervix and secured to the presenting part via a thin, spiral wire. Internal monitoring enables the provider to obtain a more accurate reading of the fetal heart rate versus an external monitor. Internal monitoring is not typically affected by movement of the laboring person or fetus.

B - _____
R - _____
A - _____
I - _____
N - _____

IUPC (Intrauterine Pressure Catheter) - The IUPC is a thin tube placed into the uterus during labor to measure the strength and frequency of contractions. The catheter is threaded into the vagina and passes through the cervix into the uterus. Unlike external contraction monitors that monitor the frequency and duration of contractions, the IUPC measures the strength of each contraction. The IUPC is not often routinely used; instead it is most commonly used when a closer and more accurate assessment of the strength of contractions becomes necessary.

B - _____
R - _____
A - _____
I - _____
N - _____

Narcotic Pain Relief - During labor, options for pain relief include narcotic based pain relievers. Typically given via intramuscular injection or via IV, narcotics such as Stadol, Nubain, Fentanyl, or Demerol can be used to decrease and alter the perception of pain by the laboring person. Due to the risk of respiratory depression in the newborn if given too close to birth, these medications are often used only in the early phase or early active phases of labor.

B - _____
R - _____
A - _____
I - _____
N - _____

Nitrous Oxide - In some birth locations, nitrous oxide may be an option for pain relief during labor. Nitrous oxide is self-administered via mask during contractions and the birthing person can choose how often and how much they inhale. The effects are short acting, typically wearing off within 5 minutes. The degree of pain relief offered by nitrous oxide is similar to that of narcotics. It is a viable alternative for those who desire pain relief but are unable to use narcotics or epidural as pain relieving options.

B - _____
R - _____
A - _____
I - _____
N - _____

Epidural Anesthesia - The epidural is a form of regional anesthesia that is given via a small catheter inserted into the epidural space between the bones of the spine. The catheter is placed in the space just outside the membrane that contains the spinal fluid and spinal cord. A continuous infusion of medication is delivered via the catheter to provide continuous pain relief during labor.

B - _____
R - _____
A - _____
I - _____
N - _____

Vacuum Delivery - Also referred to as ventouse or vacuum assisted delivery, this intervention is used during the second stage of delivery when the birthing person needs some help delivering the baby vaginally or when a quick delivery must be facilitated. The provider applies a cup or disk shaped device to the baby's head and attaches the device to a hand held vacuum pump. The pump is used to create a suction to the baby's head and traction is applied to the cup or disk via an attached handle to assist with the delivery of the baby's head while the birthing person pushes. In some cases, vacuum assisted delivery can be performed during a cesarean birth.

B - _____
R - _____
A - _____
I - _____
N - _____

Forceps Delivery - A forceps assisted delivery is facilitated by the provider using forceps that look like large spoons or salad tongs. The forceps are applied to both sides of the baby's head and connect in the middle once applied. The provider then uses the handle to apply traction and sometimes rotation to the baby's head as the birthing person pushes to facilitate a vaginal delivery.

B - _____
R - _____
A - _____
I - _____
N - _____

Cesarean Birth - A cesarean birth or cesarean delivery is a birth that is facilitated via incisions in the abdomen and uterus. Some cesarean births may be pre-planned long before labor begins; others may become necessary during the course of labor due to distress in the baby or birthing person. For most clients, they will likely be awake during the surgery.

Some medical risk factors or emergent situations may necessitate the use of general anesthesia.

B - _____
R - _____
A - _____
I - _____
N - _____

Notes:

Episiotomy

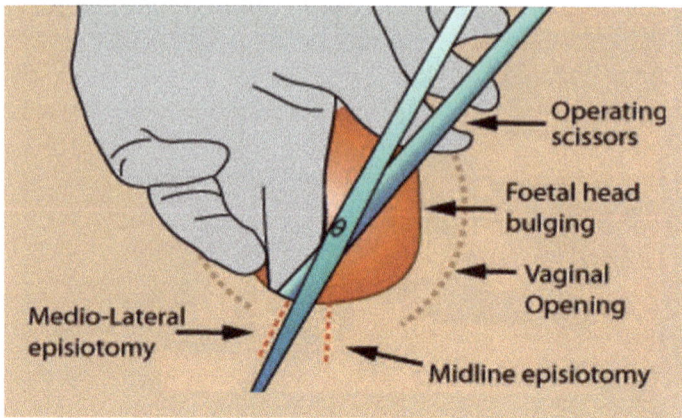

An episiotomy is a surgical incision or cut in the muscle between the vagina and the anus (known as the perineum) just prior to delivery.

This procedure was routinely done by obstetricians in order to speed delivery time and to prevent the vagina from tearing. It was thought that the straight incision of an episiotomy would heal more easily and be repaired more efficiently than a spontaneous tear.

The American Congress of Obstetricians and Gynecologists now recommends that the procedure not be done routinely. The incidence of episiotomies has been on the decline, from nearly 2 out of 3 vaginal births in 1979 to less than 5.1% in 2022.

You can potentially help your client avoid an episiotomy by encouraging them to relax the muscles of their perineum.

- Warm compresses against the perineum during the latter part of labor
- Using a warm bath during labor
- Massage on the perineum

My vagina hurts just thinking about it!

The thought of it was terrifying. Sex after a vaginal birth - are you kidding me?

I was sore. I mean really sore. It was 1992; I had an episiotomy during the birth and I was scarred for life. Literally.

The doctor put half of an open scissor inside my vagina and crunched it shut, leaving a gaping incision at the opening. After the baby was born, they sewed it up, made some sick joke about its size, and pronounced me good as new.

Good as new? I felt terrible. Oh and I forgot to mention, my partner watched in horror as the procedure took place.

I could barely walk and the idea of sitting was a joke. I was a one-cheek sitter for the first 10 days. The only thing that brought the slightest bit of comfort was that peri bottle (you know, the squirty water bottle they give you to dilute your urine when you pee). I was taking care of myself, my newborn, and my nipples, all while trying to recover from the scissor incident.

So, how can we support and prepare the perineum you ask?

The perineum is made up of muscles and muscles have memory. Leading up to your estimated due date, start enjoying a warm compress against your perineum before sexual intercourse. It is relaxing and encourages the muscles in the perineum to relax. In the later stages of labor, your doula or partner can prepare a warm compress and put it on your birth ball (exercise ball). Sit on the warm compress prior to pushing to remind those muscles to relax.

If you don't have a ball with you or you have chosen a facility to give birth in that won't allow you to get out of bed, have someone hold the warm compress against you instead. Sitting in a warm tub of water can have the same effect.

Discuss options with your provider prior to your birth regarding their comfort level with your choices. Some questions to consider discussing with your doctor or midwife in regard to this topic:

- *Do you do routine episiotomy?*
- *Can I use the tub (if there is one available to you) during my labor and birth if I choose?*
- *Will you do perineal massage during my delivery?*
- *How will you support my perineum during my delivery?*
- *Will you use medication to numb me if a repair becomes necessary?*
- *What do you recommend for pain and healing of the perineum?*

Authored by: Randy Patterson - ProDoula CEO

Epidurals

Waiting for Anesthesia

The time between when a client decides that they want an epidural and when the anesthesiologist arrives can be the most challenging part of a medicated birth. Once a client makes the decision to use medication for pain, they are done. Their resistance for pain tolerance drastically decreases. It can take between 45 minutes to an hour for the client to experience noticeable pain relief.

During this time the client is focused on one thing:

> Where is the anesthesiologist?!

Before an epidural can be placed, certain preparations must be made:

- The client must fill out a health history
- The client must be told of possible risks and sign consent
- The client must be given an IV and fluids
- An obstetrician must be "in house"
- Anesthesiologist and nurse must prep the client and the epidural site

How the doula can help during this time:

- Verbal coaching
- Deep breathing
- Vocalization
- Strong counter-pressure
- Assertive approach
- Explain the preparations and routine protocols around the epidural

Assertively coach the client to work with you to get through one contraction at a time and explain that relief is coming as quickly as possible. Remind them to "dig deep" and stay focused while the staff prepares them and the room for the procedure.

Labor Support With Epidural

For some clients an epidural is:

- Part of the plan from the beginning
- A choice that they will make in the moment

Some clients decide prior to labor that they will not include an epidural as part of their plan, but they may change their mind when labor becomes very intense.

Let's discuss ways that we can support a client who has decided to have an epidural.

Disappointment

A client who has decided to not use an epidural for labor pain management and later asks to have one may feel disappointed. They may even question their abilities or feel as though they have failed in some way. As their doula, you must support them where they are. Encourage them by validating their decisions and continuing to nurture them in the process. Listen attentively and remind them that they are making thoughtful decisions that are best for themselves during a time that is difficult to make decisions. Show your support by conveying to them that you are not disappointed in them but rather proud of their ability to make the right decision in the moment.

Fear During Administration

During the administration of the epidural, it is common for the anesthesiologist to ask the partner and the doula to step out of the room. The nurse will take on the role of "support person" during this time. Encourage your client to verbalize their fears or anxiety in relation to this to the nurse so that the nurse can provide the best comfort and support possible. If you are able to stay with your client during this time, remember that knowledge is power and the better they understand what is happening, the more comforted they may feel.

The Client's Inability to Move Legs/Lower Body

Because the epidural will make the client's lower body numb, it will be difficult for them to move. Once the medication has been evenly distributed through the body and they have rested, the doula can help by moving the client's legs and hips in order to simulate "ambulation."

The Client Mentally Detaches From Labor

Once an epidural is introduced and the client becomes relaxed and pain free, it is easy for them to "detach" from the idea that they are actually in labor and having a baby. As their doula, keeping the client engaged in discussions about birth and parenting can help them stay focused and connected to the process. This will benefit them in terms of bonding and in the postpartum weeks.

Additional Interventions Become Necessary

When an epidural is introduced other interventions typically become necessary. It is always accompanied by IV fluids, intermittent blood pressure monitoring, monitoring of one's temperature, and may require Pitocin, catheterization, and additional fetal monitoring.

Client's Ability to Push is Impaired

Due to the numbing sensation associated with the epidural, the client's ability to feel the urge to bear down may become inhibited. Without that sensation, it is difficult for the client to interpret how and when to push. With the help of the nurse, provider, and doula's coaching, the client does their best to push. If the client is still unable, they can wait to push until the medication wears off.

Inadequate Pain Relief

Unfortunately for some, epidurals don't always offer complete pain relief. Occasionally one side is more numb than the other. There may be "spots" or "windows" of pain where the epidural doesn't feel like it worked at all. Encourage the client to communicate with the anesthesiologist and nurse if this is the case. Laying in different positions can help move the medication more evenly through the body to deliver more relief.

Full Bladder, Slowing Labor

Due to the fact that the bladder sits directly below the uterus, a full bladder can prevent the baby from moving down. Keep track of when the client urinated last and, if it has been more than an hour, suggest they request the staff to empty the bladder via catheterization.

Unexpected Side Effects

Approximately 1% of individuals who choose an epidural experience a spinal headache caused by a leakage of spinal fluid. Other side effects may include shivering, ringing of the ears, backache, soreness where the needle is inserted, nausea, or difficulty urinating.

Fever, Body Temperature Elevation

For a small number of individuals, a slight fever can be associated with labor. Epidural anesthesia is known to increase the chance of this happening. Because fever is also an indication of infection, the temperature will need to be monitored in both the client and the newborn after birth.

The Client Feels Like They Can't Breathe Due to High Anesthesia Level

In some cases, during an epidural the medication moves past the breasts and up into the chest and throat. Individuals who experience this report feeling as though they cannot breathe. Because this is a terrifying sensation, it is important to remind the client that if they can talk, they can breathe. Keep them talking with you and affirming for them that they are breathing well while the medication wears off.

Once the client is "comfortable," they will likely fall asleep. Encourage the partner to get something to eat, rest, or return any necessary phone calls.

When the partner returns, you can do the same. Let the partner and their nurse know that you will be right back, but that they should call you if something changes or your client wants you back in the room.

When you return, check on the client. If they are still sleeping, you can rest quietly in a chair near the bedside or ask the nurse if there is a waiting room nearby that you may use. Again, be sure they have your cell phone number so that they are able to reach you quickly when things change.

Notes:

Epidural Quiz

The left column - numbered 1-10 - lists common side effects or symptoms that may occur during the administration of an epidural. The right column - lettered a-j - lists actions that a doula can take to assist or help with those effects and actions.

Draw a line from the number on the left-hand side to the letter on the right-hand side that corresponds to the appropriate action to take for that symptom.

1) Administration of epidural causes the client anxiety, fear, and involuntary movement.

2) The client feels disappointed about choosing an epidural.

3) The client falls asleep for a few hours.

4) The client is unable to move their legs and lower body.

5) The client seems detached from the process.

6) The client is unable to feel the urge to push and is having a difficult time figuring out how to do it.

7) The client experiences inadequate pain relief.

8) The client has a fever.

9) The client feels frightened from anesthesia rising into their chest and throat. They feel like they cannot breathe.

10) The client is feeling light headed and nauseous.

a) Take a break: call home, get a snack, and use the bathroom.

b) Cool the client down with cold washcloths on wrists, forehead, armpits, and back of the neck.

c) Explain to the client that this sensation will wear off and that if they can talk, they can breathe. Keep them talking.

d) Help the client change positions regularly.

e) Intensively coach the client to focus on relaxation. Support them with positive affirmations and remind them that they will be comfortable soon.

f) Talk with the client about the baby and their parenting philosophies. Remind them that their body and baby are working together and that they will soon be a parent!

g) Support and affirm for the client that they have made the right decision for this birth.

h) Notify the nurse or anesthesiologist while continuing to support the client through the difficult contractions.

i) Let the nurse know that your client is experiencing these sensations. Support them with cool cloths to the face and neck as the nurse addresses the underlying issue.

j) Encourage the client to let the epidural wear off a bit so that they have more feeling.

Cesarean Birth

Medical Reasons for Cesarean Birth

The following are scenarios in which a medical provider may recommend a cesarean birth. Each pregnancy is unique and one birth does not indicate how a client's next birth will unfold.

The Client Has a Medical Condition

The health care provider may recommend a cesarean birth if the client has a medical condition that could put them at risk during a trial of labor. Examples may include heart issues, high blood pressure, diabetes, or an infection that could be passed to the baby during a vaginal delivery, such as genital herpes or HIV or any number of other health risks.

In a recent discussion with Dr. Youdelman (in partnership with the Aortic Hope Association) we learned that while many of the indications for a cesarean birth above are easily recognizable, heart issues or various conditions often go unrecognized. Birthing individuals who are at increased risk for cardiovascular complications or injury such as aortic diseases or connective tissue disorders may be advised to elect for a cesarean birth.

Cardiovascular complications may occur with vaginal or cesarean deliveries, but a cesarean delivery likely has fewer hypertensive events and is advised for pregnant individuals determined to be high risk for cardiac and/or aortic injury.

Birthing individuals with a family history of cardiac and/or aortic disease or known connective tissue disorder, greatly benefit from a complete evaluation of the cardiovascular system and aorta as a part of pregnancy planning. For those with a history of cardiovascular disease/cardiovascular complications, pregnancy is considered high risk.

While there are no randomized trials on delivery methods for birthing individuals with cardiac and/or aortic disease, it is advised to utilize methods to decrease stress on the body to limit hypertension.

The Baby Has a Health Concern

A cesarean birth may be recommended if there is evidence or indication that the baby has an issue that would make a cesarean birth a safer delivery option.

Restricted Growth of the Baby

Babies who are not growing well in the womb are at a higher risk of fetal demise or of being ill at the time of birth. There is not enough evidence to show whether having a planned cesarean birth makes any difference to these risks, but it is likely that the client's provider will recommend one.

The Client Has Had a Previous Cesarean Birth

According to the American College of Obstetricians and Gynecologists, a TOLAC (trial of labor after cesarean) should be offered to most pregnant individuals during subsequent births.

Although the American College of Obstetricians and Gynecologists recommends a TOLAC, not all obstetricians/hospitals support VBAC (vaginal birth after cesarean).

The Baby Is in a Breech Position or Other "Abnormal" Position

Breech presentation, transverse fetal lie, or other compound presentations may necessitate a cesarean birth.

The Client Is Carrying Multiples

Many providers will not deliver multiples vaginally in any situation. In order for a doctor to consider vaginal delivery for multiples, both babies would ideally be in the head down position.

The Baby Is Not Getting Enough Oxygen

If the provider is concerned about the baby's oxygen supply (as indicated by changes in fetal heart tones), a cesarean birth may be recommended.

An Issue Involving the Placenta

- Placental abruption - The placenta detaches from the uterine wall prior to labor or delivery.
- Placenta previa - The placenta is close to or covering the cervix.

An Issue Involving the Umbilical Cord

- A prolapsed cord - The umbilical cord is presenting before the baby.
- The umbilical cord is being compressed by the baby/uterus during contractions.

Failure to Progress

Stalled labor is one of the most common reasons that a provider will recommend a cesarean birth. The provider will likely make this judgment based on the guidelines suggested by Friedman's Curve.

Supporting Cesarean Birth

When supporting a family through a surgical birth, a strong understanding of their personal philosophies, accompanied by your ability to attune to them, will be essential ingredients in providing the best possible support.

Each client's physical, educational, and emotional needs will be unique to the birth experience in front of them. Resist the temptation to make any assumptions regarding their thoughts about the birth. Actively listen to the client and be certain that you understand their feelings so that you can meet them where they are and assist them in processing how they feel.

Support for planned cesarean birth (this may vary based on hospital protocol and client preference):

- Speak to the client the evening before the scheduled birth
- Meet them in the parking lot of the hospital in the morning so that you can escort them to the labor and delivery unit
- Stay with them and their partner prior to the surgery
- Stay with the partner while they prep the client in the OR
- If permitted, join them in the operating room
- Meet the client in the recovery room
- Assist with infant feeding and positioning
- Answer any questions they may have
- Extend the amount of time you are present post-birth
- Follow up as normal with postpartum home visit

*If your client would like you to support them in the operating room during the birth, they will be responsible for getting the appropriate approval in order for you to do so.

Support for unplanned or emergency cesarean birth:

- In an emergency situation, time may not allow for the client to fully process the decision to move to a surgical birth
- Encourage the client to ask any and all questions they may have
- Encourage the client to ask for anything that may bring them comfort or enhance the birth experience
- Listen to the client and offer validation
- Reassure the client
- Acknowledge and validate the feelings of the client's partner
- Enable the medical providers to have access to the client by staying near the head of the bed

Selling Doula Support for a Cesarean Birth

One important aspect of educating the public is to help them understand that doula support isn't just for those who anticipate having a vaginal birth. In fact, having the support of a doula for a planned cesarean birth is just as beneficial as having one for a vaginal birth.

Regardless of how a baby is born, navigating the many choices and options available on the day of the birth can be filled with excitement, nervousness, fear, and sometimes some anxiety. Having a doula present during this time can be extremely comforting for some families.

There can be a large degree of uncertainty on the day of the surgery, or even prior to it. The client may go into labor spontaneously days or hours before, and the physical, educational, and emotional support of a doula could be very beneficial.

While scheduled cesarean births can offer a degree of planning, it is not uncommon for the time of the birth to be delayed due to an emergency.

A cesarean birth planned for 10 am may not occur until many hours later. How busy the labor and delivery unit is will be a determining factor in the time of the actual birth. Having a doula by the client's side enables the client to navigate this time of uncertainty with support and confidence.

Having the doula present after the birth is also beneficial. Navigating a newborn baby immediately post surgery can pose additional challenges that the doula can assist with. By being physically present and emotionally available, the client can ask questions, begin to process the experience, and have one-on-one support for the physical positioning of themselves and their baby.

The partner may need to step out for a few moments of self care, attend to their other children or pets, or update family members. By hiring a doula for support on the day of a cesarean birth, the clients can be assured that they will have support immediately at hand, no matter what other circumstances arise.

OB/Gyns Issue Less Restrictive VBAC Guidelines

July 21, 2010

Washington, DC -- Attempting a vaginal birth after cesarean (VBAC) is a safe and appropriate choice for most [individuals] who have had a prior cesarean delivery, including for some who have had two previous cesareans, according to guidelines released today by The American College of Obstetricians and Gynecologists.

The cesarean delivery rate in the US increased dramatically over the past four decades, from 5% in 1970 to over 31% in 2007. Before 1970, the standard practice was to perform a repeat cesarean after a prior cesarean birth. During the 1970s, as women achieved successful VBACs, it became viewed as a reasonable option for some women. Over time, the VBAC rate increased from just over 5% in 1985 to 28% by 1996, but then began a steady decline. By 2006, the VBAC rate fell to 8.5%, a decrease that reflects the restrictions that some hospitals and insurers placed on trial of labor after cesarean (TOLAC) as well as decisions by patients when presented with the risks and benefits.

"The current cesarean rate is undeniably high and absolutely concerns us as OB/GYNs," said Richard N. Waldman, MD, president of The College. "These VBAC guidelines emphasize the need for thorough counseling of benefits and risks, shared patient-doctor decision making, and the importance of patient autonomy. Moving forward, we need to work collaboratively with our patients and our colleagues, hospitals, and insurers to swing the pendulum back to fewer cesareans and a more reasonable VBAC rate."

In keeping with past recommendations, most [individuals] with one previous cesarean delivery with a low-transverse incision are candidates for and should be counseled about VBAC and offered a TOLAC. In addition, "The College guidelines now clearly say that [individuals] with two previous low-transverse cesarean incisions, [those] carrying twins, and [individuals] with an unknown type of uterine scar are considered appropriate candidates for a TOLAC," said Jeffrey L. Ecker, MD, from Massachusetts General Hospital in Boston and immediate past Vice Chair of the Committee on Practice Bulletins-Obstetrics who co-wrote the document with William A. Grobman, MD, from Northwestern University in Chicago.

VBAC Counseling on Benefits and Risks

"In making plans for delivery, physicians and patients should consider a [person's] chance of a successful VBAC as well as the risk of complications from a trial of labor, all viewed in the context of [their] future reproductive plans," said Dr. Ecker. Approximately 60-80% of appropriate candidates who attempt VBAC will be successful. A VBAC avoids major abdominal surgery, lowers a person's risk of hemorrhage and infection, and shortens postpartum recovery. It may also help them avoid the possible future risks of having multiple cesareans such as hysterectomy, bowel and bladder injury, transfusion, infection, and abnormal placenta conditions (placenta previa and placenta accreta).

Both repeat cesarean and a TOLAC carry risks including maternal hemorrhage, infection, operative injury, blood clots, hysterectomy, and death. Most maternal injury that occurs during a TOLAC happens when a repeat cesarean becomes necessary after the TOLAC fails. A successful VBAC has fewer complications than an elective repeat cesarean while a failed TOLAC has more complications than an elective repeat cesarean.

Uterine Rupture

The risk of uterine rupture during a TOLAC is low — between 0.5% and 0.9% — but if it occurs, it is an emergency situation. A uterine rupture can cause serious injury to a person and their baby. The College maintains that a TOLAC is most safely undertaken where staff can immediately provide an emergency cesarean, but recognizes that such resources may not be universally available.

"Given the onerous medical liability climate for OB-GYNS, interpretation of The College's earlier guidelines led many hospitals to refuse allowing VBACs altogether," said Dr. Waldman.

"Our primary goal is to promote the safest environment for labor and delivery, not to restrict [an individual's] access to VBAC."

Birthing individuals and their physicians may still make a plan for a TOLAC in situations where there may not be "immediately available" staff to handle emergencies, but it requires a thorough discussion of the local health care system, the available resources, and the potential for incremental risk. "It is absolutely critical that [the individual and their] physician discuss VBAC early in the prenatal care period so that logistical plans can be made well in advance," said Dr. Grobman. And those hospitals that lack "immediately available" staff should develop a clear process for gathering them quickly and all hospitals should have a plan in place for managing emergency uterine ruptures, however rarely they may occur, Dr. Grobman added.

The College says that restrictive VBAC policies should not be used to force individuals to undergo a repeat cesarean delivery against their will if, for example, a person in labor presents for care and declines a repeat cesarean delivery at a center that does not support TOLAC. On the other hand, if, during prenatal care, a physician is uncomfortable with a patient's desire to undergo VBAC, it is appropriate to refer them to another physician or center.

(Source: Practice Bulletin #115, "Vaginal Birth after Previous Cesarean Delivery," is published in the August 2010 issue of Obstetrics & Gynecology)

Breech Positions Described

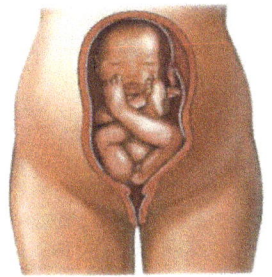 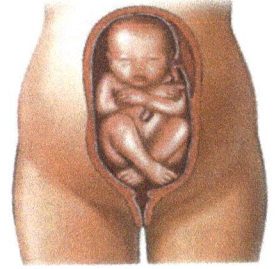 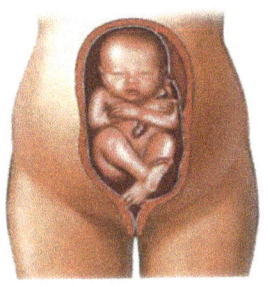

Frank Complete Footling

Frank breech - The baby's bottom comes first. Their legs are flexed at the hips and extended at the knees (with feet near the ears); 65–70% of breech babies are in the frank breech position.

Complete breech - The baby's hips and knees are flexed so that the baby is sitting cross legged, with feet beside the bottom.

Footling breech- One or both of the baby's feet come first, with the baby's bottom at a higher position; this is rare at term but relatively common with premature fetuses.

Natural & Medical Options a Client Can Explore When the Baby is Breech

A client who is anticipating a vaginal birth who later learns that their baby is in a breech position can be very disappointed and may seek out options for turning the baby.

The role of a doula does not include utilizing techniques to turn a breech baby. However, supporting someone as they make choices regarding what they will do in this scenario is.

The following is a list of common techniques that you should be aware of that are used to turn babies to the head down position.

Headstand in the Water - This activity is most effective when performed often and should never be done without the physical support of another adult nearby.

Breech Tilt - Performed 3 times daily for 10-15 minutes each time, with an empty stomach and when the baby is active. Prop one end of an ironing board securely on a sofa or chair 12-18" high (or may use slant board). The individual will lie down with bent knees while keeping their feet flat on the board. They should relax, breathe deeply, and avoid tensing. They may also use pillows on a flat surface to raise their hips 12-18" above shoulders. Gravity may help the baby get into a head down position.

Pelvic Tilt - While lying on the back, with knees flexed and feet on the floor, place three large pillows under the buttocks and apply an ice pack to the top of the belly. This works best on an empty stomach and is recommended to do for 10 minutes, twice a day. Try this in conjunction with headphones and visualization.

Knee-chest position - Kneel with hips flexed slightly more than 90 degrees while making sure that the thighs are not pressing against the belly. Combine with placing shoulders and upper chest flat on a mattress for 15 minutes every two waking hours, for 5 consecutive days.

The following techniques will require the assistance of a professional:

Moxibustion – A form of traditional Chinese medicine that involves burning a mugwort stick near a certain point on the small toe of the foot. Refer to an acupuncturist for this.

Acupuncture - Find an acupuncturist who is familiar with pregnancy and knows the points to stimulate for turning a breech baby.

Webster Breech Technique - Sacral manipulation and abdominal effleurage performed by a chiropractor trained in this technique.

External Cephalic Version – An External Cephalic Version can be done in the hospital at about 37 weeks. It is a procedure that is used to turn the baby from breech to head down using external pressure on the baby's head and bottom to rotate them in the uterus. The provider may give medication to keep the uterus relaxed during the procedure. Some providers may also prefer that an epidural be utilized for the procedure. In this case, if the procedure is successful an induction of labor may be the next step. If the procedure is not successful the provider will move to a cesarean delivery utilizing the epidural as anesthesia for the surgery. Refer the client to their care provider for more specific information for their individual process. If you are present for this procedure, your role will be one of grounding, reassurance, and helping the client to utilize focused relaxation techniques.

Challenging Childbirth

When Birth Plans Fall Short

Disappointment, doubt, frustration, anger, resentment, and a host of other negative feelings may reveal themselves to a client who has set certain expectations for their birth and then is denied those expectations. During the labor as things unfold, focus on the parts of the "plan" that are able to occur. Those things may be as simple as:

- "Your body went into labor on its own."
- "Your partner doesn't have to leave your side."
- "You are able to decide when you have a vaginal exam."

Reminding your clients of these things will help keep them focused and hopefully fulfilled by their experience. Refrain from saying things like:

- "At least your baby is healthy."
- "At least you didn't have to feel any contractions."
- "You should be grateful that you and the baby are ok."

Friends and family members outside of the birth world may say these things thinking that they are encouraging this new parent. These comments are not empowering and typically do not make them feel better. They can sometimes be guilt producing for the client instead. The client may have to work through mourning the loss of the experience they hoped for and as a doula, you can support them through this process. An experience such as this can also lead to postpartum depression and other postpartum mood and anxiety disorders. The client may need professional support beyond a doula's code of conduct.

The Role of a Doula During an Emergency

In an emergency situation you must remember that your role is support. As doulas, we are not trained medical professionals and can offer no advice or assistance in the context of an emergency.

However, our role is important. Keeping a client relaxed and calm in a crisis will help them feel safe and can help them maintain their composure while the medical team is addressing the emergency.

Support your client by:

- Staying calm.
- Not being in the way of the providers.
- Speaking in a direct and comforting way.
  - "You are doing great."
  - "You have chosen all of the right people to take care of you and your baby."
  - "You have built an amazing team."
  - "Slow your breathing."
- Explaining what is going on to the client and/or their partner in the event of a true emergency. The client may not be given options regarding their wishes during a true emergency. As the doula, you may help them process this scenario once the baby has been born and the client is recovering.

An individual may experience birth trauma due to unexpected scenarios and may require professional support beyond what a doula can provide.

Immediate Postpartum and the Newborn

Continuous Support

Once the baby is born, the client still has work to do. Although they are relieved and thrilled to meet their baby, they must still deliver the placenta, be examined, be "repaired" if necessary, and be cleaned up.

As the doula, you will continue to support the client through these uncomfortable procedures. Continue to coach and affirm them while reminding them to use the breathing techniques or coping methods that they used during labor for pain management.

Often the focus of the "team" shifts to the baby after delivery. The client is still your number one priority. When the doctor or midwife has finished, help the nurse get the client cleaned up and comfortable. Ask if it is okay to order them something to eat and ask the client if there are any personal items in their bag that you can get for them such as a toothbrush, lip balm, hair brush, comfort item, etc.

The Golden Hour

The American Academy of Pediatrics (AAP) policy on The Golden Hour recommends new guidelines for how a newborn and their parents should be treated in the first hour after birth.

The creation of the policy was prompted in response to the outdated practices immediately post birth which may interfere with a baby's transition to extrauterine life and their potential impact on the initiation of breastfeeding.

The guidelines as written by the American Academy of Pediatrics are as follows:

- Healthy infants should be placed immediately onto the abdomen or chest when they are born and remain in direct skin-to-skin contact until the first feeding is accomplished.
- The nurse should perform the first physical assessment while the baby remains on the chest.
- Weighing, measuring, bathing, eye ointment, and any injections or blood tests should wait until after the first feeding.
- The baby should remain with the [client] throughout the recovery

period.

Source: American Academy of Pediatrics

Family Bonding

Always be observant and respectful of the family bond. As doulas, we do our best to understand the attachment needs of the families that we serve. However, we cannot always understand the personal and intimate dynamics of our client's relationships. Stay aware and consider what they may need. Remember to give them "space" to bond as a family. When appropriate, step out and give them a few moments of privacy. Linger outside of the room, letting them know you are just outside if they need you.

Celebrate and affirm their connection verbally, while also respecting those private moments.

Often it becomes obvious about 1-2 hours after the birth that the family is ready to settle in and truly bond as a family. The doula should instinctively know that it is time to say good-bye when this happens.

APGAR

Virginia Apgar, (7 June 1909 – 7 August 1974), was an American pediatric anesthesiologist. She was a leader in the fields of anesthesiology, teratology, and effectively founded the field of neonatology.

To the public, however, she is best known as the developer of the APGAR score. A method of assessing the health of newborn babies that has drastically reduced infant mortality over the world.

Dr. Apgar was a professor of anesthesia at Columbia University when during breakfast one day, a medical student rotating through the obstetric anesthesia program stated that there should be a way to evaluate newborns. Dr. Apgar immediately grabbed the nearest piece of paper and quickly jotted down what was to become the 5 points of the APGAR score. Then she ran off to the labor and delivery unit to try it out.

What followed was a collaboration of research assistants and physicians coming together to refine the system. Dr. Apgar published it in 1953. It wasn't until 1963 that the epigram of APGAR was given to the score to help medical staff remember the 5 points.

Dr. Apgar's method of structured thinking and creating a model for clinical assessments was the catalyst for other clinical assessment structures, such as the Glasgow Coma Score and the Trauma Score.

There are 2 widely used acronyms that are derived from Dr. Apgar's name.

- American Pediatric Gross Assessment Record
- Appearance, Pulse, Grimace, Activity, Respiration

APGAR scoring system. Each category is scored with a 0, 1, or 2, with 2 being the strongest rating. The numbers are then totaled with 10 being considered a perfect score.

APGAR Score			
Sign/Score	0	1	2
Appearance (skin color)	Blue or Pale	Body pink, extremities blue	Pink
Pulse Rate (heart rate)	None	Less than 100 beats per minute	Greater than 100 beats per minute
Grimace (reflex irritability)	None	Grimace	Cries
Activity (muscle tone)	Limp	Arms and legs flexed	Active movement
Respiration (breathing)	Absent	Slow/irregular	Good, strong cry

APGARs are done at one and five minutes post birth:

- The one minute APGAR determines how well the baby tolerated the birth process.
- The five minute APGAR tells the doctor how well the baby is doing outside of the client's womb.

The Basics of Early Bodyfeeding

As a labor doula it is not expected that you will know everything about chest or breastfeeding. It is expected that you will be able to "support" a client who is bodyfeeding, particularly in the very early stages.

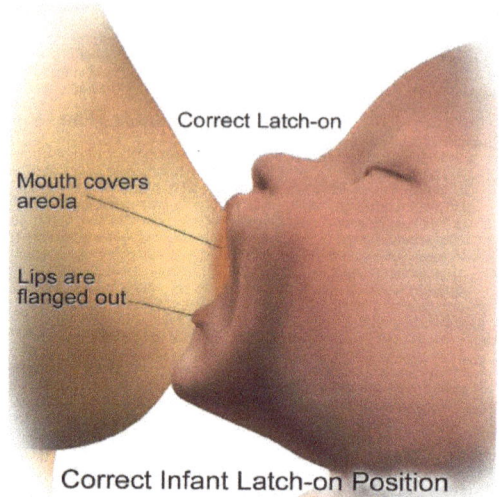

Correct Infant Latch-on Position

Chest or breastfeeding in the early moments post-birth will vary, as each client and their baby is unique. A baby who is "bubbling" mucus and fluid will need to work through that before being ready to feed. Some babies take a few moments to get used to breathing before they become ready to find the breast or chest. During this time, you can assure the client that it is perfectly normal for the baby to take their time and come to the body on their own.

Breast Crawl

The term breast crawl was first coined in 1998 by Marshall Klaus. This term describes an organized group of behaviors that can be seen in healthy newborns in the first hours of life.

After birth the newborn is dried off and placed immediately on the birthing parent's chest. A short while later the newborn will begin rooting and sucking. As the infant roots, they raise and lower their heads, allowing them to visually identify the nipple. They will then begin to lean and continue to root in the direction of the nipple. They will continue to root and raise and lower their heads until they come into alignment with the nipple and self attach.

According to www.breastcrawl.org the breast crawl is described as:

"Immediately after birth the child was dried and laid on the [birthing parent's] chest. In the control group a regular behavioural sequence, previously not described in the literature, was observed. After 15 minutes of comparative inactivity, spontaneous sucking and rooting movements occurred, reaching maximal intensity at 45 minutes. The first hand-to-mouth movement was observed at a mean of 34± 2 minutes after birth and at 55+ minutes the infant spontaneously found the nipple and started to suckle."

Feeding cues

- Mouth opening
- Lip smacking
- Rooting – head turning, nuzzling, seeking the nipple by raising and lowering the head, bobbing
- Hand to mouth

Proper Latch

A proper latch at the breast or chest should include the following:

- The baby's lips should be "flanged" as shown in the diagram.
- The baby's mouth should cover the majority of the areola.
- The nipple should be against the soft palate of the baby's mouth.

The bodyfeeding parent should be comfortable:

- Their shoulders should be in a relaxed position.
- They should sit or lay comfortably with pillows for propping and supporting them if necessary.
- There should be no pain once the baby is sucking and swallowing.

Bodyfeeding Positions

The Cradle Hold – The baby's head is cradled in the crook of the arm. The baby and parent are belly to belly, nose to nipple and the baby is brought to the body. The breast or chest can be supported and/or manipulated with the opposite hand.

The Cross Cradle Hold – The baby is in the same position as described above, however, the parent switches their hands. The hand opposite the breast that the baby is feeding on wraps over the baby for support. The baby's head is in the parents hand. The hand on the same side of the body that the baby is feeding on can support and manipulate the breast.

The Side-Lying Position – The parent is lying on their side with the baby facing them and uses their lower arm to cradle the baby's back. The baby is nose to nipple and brought to the breast or chest.

The Football Hold - The baby is cradled, facing upward, in the parent's arm. With their arm and palm of their hand supporting the baby's body, neck, and head, the baby is nestled closely against the client's side. The baby's feet and legs should be tucked under the client's arm and the baby is lifted to the chest or breast.

Breaking the Latch

To take the baby off the breast, the client must break the suction of the latch by inserting a finger into the corner of the baby's mouth before pulling the baby away.

Knowing When to Call an Expert

An International Board Certified Lactation Consultant (IBCLC) is the appropriate medical professional that a client should be referred to when experiencing chest or breastfeeding issues. Reasons to refer to an IBCLC include:

- The latch is consistently shallow
- The client is experiencing pain
- There is severe nipple soreness
- The baby is not gaining weight
- There is a suspected low milk supply
- The client is experiencing anxiety regarding feedings
- The baby has a persistent difficulty latching
- The client desires more information or support than you can provide

Newborn Medications

Erythromycin and Vitamin K are two medications that are offered to newborns within the first hour of life.

Erythromycin is a mineral oil and white petroleum based antibiotic ointment that is placed in and on the newborn's eyes. This is done to protect the baby from potentially acquiring an infection during the birth process. In many areas, the administration of this medication is state mandated.

If a family is not comfortable with this medication being given to their newborn, encourage them to learn of their options prior to giving birth and properly execute those options upon the birth of their baby.

Vitamin-K is an injection given to newborns shortly after birth. Without it, they do not have the ability to clot their own blood during the first week of life. In many areas the administration of this medication is state mandated.

If a family is not comfortable with this medication being given to their child, encourage them to learn of their options prior to giving birth and properly execute those options upon the birth of their child.

Hepatitis-B vaccine is offered to newborns shortly after birth. The early immunization of Hepatitis-B is not mandated in most states at this time.

Families may choose to immunize their baby against Hepatitis-B within the first hour post birth, or they may make this decision with their pediatrician at a later time. If a family chooses to decline this vaccine, the client will be required to sign a form stating their choice.

Postpartum Follow-Up Visit

The postpartum follow-up visit is an appointment scheduled shortly after the client returns home from the hospital or in the case of a home birth, a few days after the baby is born. This appointment is an opportunity to check in with the client, see if they are in need of additional support or resources, and finalize the doula support contract.

Prior to the client leaving the hospital, follow up with them by phone.

- Mention a specific detail from the labor.
- Compliment them with specific details.
  - "When you closed your eyes and started rocking, I knew you were in the zone! You were awesome."
  - "Your movements during labor, especially during transition, were so graceful and confident. You were magnificent to watch."
- Plan a visit within one week of the client coming home.
- If you have spoken by phone or email and they are struggling with something (breastfeeding, issue with the baby, etc.), remember to inquire about how things are going in relation to your previous conversation with them during your visit.

Keep in mind that scheduling an appointment during the early days of the postpartum period can be a bit overwhelming and may seem unimportant to a client who is exhausted and trying to keep up with the changing needs of a newborn.

When scheduling this appointment, it is perfectly acceptable to say something along the lines of, "If you don't have any appointments on Tuesday, I can be there around 11:00. Does that work for you?"

When arriving to the scheduled visit, be sure to do the following:

- Be on time.
- Wash your hands.
- If it seems appropriate, ask to hold the baby.
  - If it is clear that the parent and baby are "nesting" together - working on feeding, snuggling, bonding - do not interrupt that time together by asking to hold the baby.
- Offer some focus and attention to any siblings.
- Ask questions.

- "How is it going?"
- "Sleeping?"
- "Feeding?"
- Find out if they are struggling with anything in particular.
- Offer support if they are breast or chest feeding and having challenges. Look at the baby's latch and offer some affirmation and encouragement.
- Ask about swaddling and pacifiers. Talk about it in relation to sleep. When you do it correctly, it can be life changing for them. Offer to swaddle the baby and let them video it.
- Encourage them to talk about the birth. Listen and answer any questions they may have.
- Be complementary and encouraging.
- If the partner is there, include them too. Talk about their experience.
- Remind them to call if they need additional support.
- Follow up with any resources they might need.
- Periodically connect through cards, emails, or social media.

Doula Self Care

Processing the Birth

As a doula you are sharing in another person's intimate birth experience. Although the experience does not belong to you, you may have thoughts or feelings in regard to it that you need to process.

It is important that you address these feelings prior to attending another birth, as they may have great influence on you when you are placed in the birth setting again.

There are several steps to processing your emotions.

1. Become aware that you are having an emotional experience.
2. Name the feelings that you are having appropriately.
3. Understand what caused you to have these emotions.
4. Evaluate the impact these feelings have had on you.
5. Decide how you will cope with or deal with your feelings.

Often it takes support to work through these steps. You may not be able to do it alone. Reach out to other doulas, a mentor, the team at ProDoula, or, if necessary, a professional to be certain that you are ready to support your next client without any potentially negative repercussions.

The Life of a Doula

When we think of becoming a doula we are thrilled at the opportunity to support and encourage other people through the journey of birth and parenthood. We are passionate and enthusiastic, but we must also be committed and accountable.

Our clients depend on us. They have expectations of us and we must not disappoint them. Think about what being "on call" looks like for you.

- Do you have young children?
- A demanding "other" job?
- Family members relying on you?
- Pets relying on you?

Remember that you may be called to a birth and unavailable to your other responsibilities for many hours. Ask yourself these questions:

- Am I prepared to commit to this?
- Do I have the support I need to commit to this?
    - Childcare or rides for my children
    - A care provider for my children if they are ill
    - A supportive partner (if applicable)
- Do I understand what total commitment to being "on call" means?

Consider a "Shared Call Schedule"

Find another doula that you are compatible with and work as a team.

Explain to potential clients that you share a call schedule with a partner and the client will meet the two of you together. If they decide to move forward with the two of you, they will meet with both of you prenatally, and the one of you that is on call when they go into labor will be the one who will attend the birth.

The Benefits of Shared Call

For the client – The client never has to worry about having a "back-up" doula whom they have not met or one that may be disappointing to them. They can be confident that one of the two of you WILL attend their birth. They will have had the opportunity to get to know both of you and will feel comfortable with either of you supporting them. They have shared their thoughts, fears, concerns, and excitement about their birth with both of you and they are comforted by the idea that their team is in place.

For the doulas – Each doula will be on call for about 15 days a month, unless their schedules don't allow for that. In a case such as this, one doula may be on call for more days than the other and financial arrangements should reflect that. Scheduling personal appointments can be done on the days that each doula is not "on call" and their life can maintain some predictability. They can be prepared with personal systems in place on their call days and live their normal life on their off call days.

When on call:

- Your phone should always be charged and near you
- You must not consume any mind or mood altering substances,

including alcohol
- You must always have reliable and efficient transportation
- You must be within an appropriate distance to your client and the birth facility of choice
- You must be prepared to leave your own life and become part of the client's for however many hours are required of you
  - Gas in your car
  - Money for parking
  - A bag packed and ready
  - Childcare in place, etc.

Entry Level Business for Doulas

While you were probably eagerly awaiting this training so you could become a doula, you may not feel so excited about becoming a business owner. But don't worry - ProDoula is committed to supporting you as you begin this new chapter. In addition to the support from the Training & Development Team and the Home Office, there are numerous resources available to you on the ProDoula website, www.prodoula.com.

On the website, you can find various resources to get your business off the ground and help it succeed, from business plan templates to Advanced Business Training webinars to individualized business consulting with ProDoula CEO, author, and entrepreneur, Randy Patterson. Resources are available to you throughout any stage of your business journey.

ProDoula's Doula Learning Channel (www.doulalearningchannel.com) also provides you with comprehensive, enriching courses for both practical and business continuing education. Your training and certifying organization is here to ensure you have the tools and knowledge to run a successful doula business - remember to reach out and utilize these things.

Starting a Doula Business - What You Will Need

A Business Name

Before you can complete some of the following tasks, you will need to settle on a name for your business. Remember to take into account the importance of things like branding and search engine optimization (SEO), rather than what personally appeals to you, when deciding on a name for your new business.

ProDoula's Advanced Business Training or private business consulting with ProDoula's CEO, Randy Patterson, can assist you with creating a brand, including a name and logo, if you need help in this area.

Business Structure

Regardless of whether you will work as an independent doula, open a doula agency, or work as an independent contractor, you must establish your business under a recognized legal structure for your state. This might be a Limited Liability Company (LLC), an S-Corporation (S-Corp), or Doing Business As (DBA). Enlist the help of a professional, such as an attorney or an accountant, to determine which is the right structure for you. This is the first step to legitimizing your business and will set you up to pay taxes as such.

In most states you will need to have a recognized legal business structure before you can apply for an Employer Identification Number (EIN) or open a business bank account, both of which are important for a professional doula business.

What Doula Business Model Is Right For You?

Become An Independent Doula

This will allow you to make your own rules. You will decide how many clients you will serve, how you will market and sell your services, and what those services will be. With the freedom and flexibility to make all of your own rules comes responsibility and pressure that can be overwhelming or unfamiliar.

ProDoula will help you navigate and overcome these challenges by:

- Offering you strategies, support, and systems that will contribute to your confidence.
- Providing advice on establishing your business and creating the balance that is right for you and your family.
- Making the necessary courses and consultations available to you as you develop and grow your business.

Own A Doula Agency

For the entrepreneur-turned-doula or doula-turned-entrepreneur, this is a rewarding opportunity, both personally and financially.

It puts you in the driver's seat, setting an agency agenda and becoming a leader. In this scenario, you are responsible for your own financial success, but you also contribute to the financial success of the independent contractors that your agency offers work to. It can be stressful and overwhelming but also incredibly rewarding.

ProDoula can provide a tremendous amount of support and advice by:

- Sharing the company history of Northeast Doulas – the successful

doula agency established by the founders of ProDoula.
- Providing guidance on how to find, train, and inspire doulas.
- Guiding you on how to set up the relationship – financially as well as the legal structure and business flow of information.
- Providing templates for contracts between your business and clients and subcontractor.
- Providing strategies and resources for various marketing and network strategies necessary to keep your doulas working.
- And so much more!

Work For An Agency

Consider working for a doula agency as an employee or independent contractor. This type of work allows you to work for clients without any of the time or expenses associated with finding those clients. You will be paid for the time you are working, although at a rate that is lower than what you would earn as an independent doula.

ProDoula can provide you guidance to:

- Establish all necessary legal/financial protections for yourself – setting up LLC, insurance, etc.
- Establish boundaries and clear communication with the agency owner.
- Negotiate pay/terms and conditions of contract with the agency.

Decide on Pricing

Setting the fee for your service is one of the most important decisions you will make for your doula business. The prices you begin with can either support your future growth or hold you back.

Do not allow others or your own negative thinking deter you from charging fair and competitive compensation for your dedication and service to your clients. Your investment of time, money, and personal sacrifice deserves to be compensated.

A largely debated topic is the decision to include or exclude prices on your website. While this is certainly an individual decision, it is important to remember that expectant families are not just buying a doula. They are buying a relationship with a doula. Regardless of how well written your website is, without having a discussion by phone or in-person with you, the individual can not determine whether or not you are worth the price listed. For that reason, ProDoula recommends that you do not list your prices on your website but rather discuss them with the potential client when speaking with them.

Insurance Coverage/Reimbursement

As doula support becomes more mainstream, increasingly companies are offering benefits that cover or reimburse for doula services, such as Carrot Fertility. Some states are even including doula coverage in their Medicaid benefits. These options can allow more people to benefit from doula support, however, it is important to consider what this will require of you as a business owner.

Companies that reimburse for doula services will normally create their own requirements for which doula services are eligible. Almost all require that the doula be certified. Some list specific training organizations, while others will establish a certain number of hours of training that must be completed. If you think you will work with clients using insurance benefits or Medicaid, it is very important to complete your certification. You may also want to pursue additional advanced trainings, such as ProDoula's Advanced Comfort Measures for Labor or ProDoula's Labor Doula Master Class, to ensure that you have sufficient learning to meet their requirements.

Another option that some clients might have for reimbursement is through their FSA or HSA benefits. If you are equipped to run credit card transactions for your business, then you will likely be able to process these payments. You may need to instruct your clients to check with their company's benefits manager to see if there are any specific details that should be included on the labor doula invoice to make sure that the support is covered.

A Website

In today's day and age, you NEED a website if clients are going to find you. If your budget allows, you can hire a professional web designer to build one for you. Otherwise, you can create your own website.

There are numerous DIY website platforms such as:

- Wordpress

- Squarespace
- Wix

All of these platforms offer easy-to-use templates to help you create a website with great SEO. ProDoula CEO, Randy Patterson, also offers affordable copywriting services to help you get your website published as quickly as possible.

Your website does not have to be complex, however there are a few essential pages that you will want to consider including.

Homepage - Your Homepage is a potential client's first impression of your business. Since this can easily be the only page they visit before leaving, be sure to give a clear overall understanding of what you offer. This page should speak in your "brand's voice" and include an overview of your services, with links and language that encourage prospective clients to explore your website further. Be sure to have a call to action (link to contact you) on this page and all others.

About Page - Your About Page is where you can express your mission statement, share a statement of inclusivity, and feature yourself and your expertise to prospective clients. This is the place to share more about yourself, what drew you to doula work, your training and experience, as well as some personal anecdotes.

Services Page - Your Services Page is where you will feature a more in depth description of the supportive services that you offer prospective clients. It is best to focus on the benefits of what you provide versus the features. Utilize language here that paints a picture of how your services can enhance the client's experience.

Contact Page - Your Contact Page is the place where prospective clients can inquire further about your services. Consider the information that you would like to know about this person and include it on the contact form. Keep in mind that requiring too much information before connecting with someone may deter them from contacting you at all. Keep it simple by asking for basic information such as:

- Name
- Phone number
- Email
- Due date

Blog Page - Your Blog Page is one of the best and most effective ways to increase your ranking in search engine results for doulas in your community. It is also a great opportunity to expose your community to the voice of your brand, your expertise, and further paint a picture of the type of support you offer and how they benefit your clients.

Get Doula Insurance

Although there is no legal structure from state to state regarding insurance for doulas, ProDoula strongly advises that you protect yourself and your assets with an insurance policy.

Currently, you are able to purchase doula insurance through CM&F Group Inc.

Contact them to apply for this very affordable coverage before beginning work as a doula.

Call the information center at CM&F: 800.221.4904. Or, visit them online for more information: https://www.cmfgroup.com

In Canada: LMS Prolink: http://www.lmsprolink.ca/ or 800.663.6828.

Create Contracts

Many business deals call for the creation of a written contract. A contract is a legal document that is designed to protect the parties involved from fraud and poor business practices. Hiring a lawyer to write or design a contract, while important, is often expensive and time consuming. Thus, many people choose to write their own contracts. Contracts are recognized and used in a court system because they are considered legal documents.

Therefore, you should always use care when you write a contract

6 Tips For Writing Your Contract:

- Word contracts simply and avoid unnecessary legal jargon.
- List penalties and consequences if the agreement is not fulfilled.
- Declare the monetary terms clearly.
- Include the names, addresses, and telephone numbers for the contracting parties.
- Clearly include the date of commencement on the contract.

- Create an area for signatures and dates of all parties engaging in the contract.

ProDoula provides you with the following Labor Doula Support Contract to use as a template for your own business. The below contract is intended for a solo labor doula that is practicing with a back up doula in place. It can be edited to fit your business model. For example, be sure to edit paragraph 8 if you work with an Agency or doula partnership that practices a shared call schedule.

Labor Doula Support Contract

This Contract is between the birthing parent and partner (hereinafter referred to as "Client"), and [Insert Doula's Name/Business Name] (hereinafter referred to as "Doula") for the purposes of providing labor doula support. After discussion and review, the parties agree as follows:

I. The Prenatal Visit:

1. Doula will provide one visit prior to the birth (hereinafter referred to as the "Prenatal Visit") at which Client shall discuss a proposed birth plan that reflects Client's needs and desires.

II. The Doula:

2. Doula works for Client.

3. Doula has the necessary skills and training so as to enable Doula to perform the services for which the labor doula has been contracted. Doula will support Client's decisions within the limits of Doula's code of conduct.

4. Doula will articulate and explain all available options and birth plan choices during the Prenatal Visit.

5. Doula will remain with Client once active labor has begun, or earlier, as requested by Client.

6. Doula will NOT perform any medical procedures or make decisions regarding medical care for Client and/or baby, as this is outside Doula's code of conduct.

7. Doula will be on call 24 hours a day starting upon execution of contract by Client.

8. Doula will be responsible for providing a qualified, professional back up doula in the unlikely event Doula cannot attend the birth. Client shall have the right to meet with back up doula if they so choose.

9. Doula shall strive to create a calm and peaceful environment within the circumstances allowed by the birth location.

10. Doula will remain with Client until at least one hour after the birth of the baby.

11. Doula will provide a one-hour follow up postpartum visit within 10 days after the birth of the baby. At this meeting, Doula will answer any and all questions regarding the birth and care of the newborn. Additional postpartum services can be arranged through Doula or Doula can refer Client to a qualified and professional Postpartum & Infant Care Doula.

Client Initials _____

III. Client Responsibilities:

12. Client agrees to contact Doula at the onset of labor. Client will advise where Doula should report to begin in-person labor support. Doula will report within 2 hours of Client's request.

13. It is Client's responsibility to contact Doula by TELEPHONE when Client believes labor has begun. This is the only appropriate channel to communicate with Doula regarding labor support; texts, emails, or social media messages will not suffice. Any requests made to Doula to begin in-person labor support NOT made by TELEPHONE will be insufficient to trigger Doula's responsibilities for the purposes of this contract.

IV. Additional Protocols:

14. In the event there is a public emergency (severe weather, public health pandemic, etc.) at the time Doula's in-person physical support is requested and local government has advised the public to shelter in place or remain off public roads or area hospitals are closed to doulas, Doula shall provide virtual support to Client via Zoom, FaceTime, or other similar video chat platform during the labor and delivery and up to 1 hour postpartum. See Virtual Labor Support Addendum.

15. In the event Client is positive for Covid 19 or one of its variants at the time they request Doula's in-person physical support, Doula shall provide virtual support to Client via Zoom, FaceTime, or other similar video chat platform during the labor and delivery and up to 1 hour postpartum. See Virtual Labor Support Addendum. Client may schedule the postpartum follow-up visit virtually or wait until they have received a negative PCR test to schedule the in person visit with Doula.

V. Fee for Services:

16. The fee for labor support is $____. [Insert labor doula fee] This payment amount includes one prenatal visit, 1 postpartum follow-up visit (limited to 1 hour), unlimited phone, text, or email support, and 12 hours of face-to face-labor support. This fee is due at the time of contract signing. Failure to make the agreed upon payment will render this contract null and void. Please note that once this contract is executed all fees are non-refundable.

17. Additional labor support beyond the 12 contracted face-to-face hours will be billed at the rate of $___ per hour. [Insert hourly rate] Client is responsible to pay for any and all parking fees incurred by Doula. These fees will be billed after services are rendered and payment is expected within 14 days of billing.

18. Doula cannot guarantee the type of labor and birth Client will have. Doula will not refund or negotiate fees based on the circumstances surrounding birth, including medical determinations regarding labor and delivery.

19. Should Client fail to notify Doula by telephone TWO hours prior to the requested report time and Doula misses the birth, the full fee will be retained by Doula.

20. The full fee of $____ [Insert fee here] will be refunded if Doula misses the birth as a result of reporting to the birth more than two hours after Client's request.

21. We, the undersigned, have read this Labor Support Contract. We accept and agree to the terms and conditions.

Client Initials _____

Birthing Parent (Printed Name) _____
Birthing Parent Signature _____
Partner (Printed Name) _____
Partner Signature _____
Address: _____
Phone Numbers: _____
Emails: _____
Due Date: _____

Birthing Facility: _____
_____
_____

Doula (Printed Name) _____
Business Name _____
Address: _____
Phone: _____
Email: _____

Business Forms

There is no shortage of help on the Internet for people starting a new business. From business plans to profit and loss statements, most templates are available for free and are easy to download.

The truth is, that in order to start your business, you do not need complicated forms or software applications. For the first few years you will want to spend as much time as possible with clients or potential clients and as little time on the computer doing administrative work as you can.

The Client Intake Call

It is important to capture potential customer information when someone calls you and inquires about you or your business. During your intake call be sure to take notes regarding pertinent information.

The Art of the Intake Call

The intake call is often the doula's first chance to demonstrate what it is like to have the supportive care of a doula. The intention of this call is connection. Show the potential client through their interactions with you what it feels like to have you by their side, providing information and support from the start.

These calls will typically last between 30-40 minutes. During the call, focus on building a relationship with the individual on the other end of the phone. Be mindful and intentional about what experience you want the person to have during the call.

Tracking Form

It is important to track customers through each step of your business relationship with them. At times you may want to compare customer information or group the information by month, service type, etc. This is why we recommend that you use Excel, Google Sheets, or a similar program.

Income Statement

An income statement, or profit and loss statement, is a financial statement that summarizes a company's revenues and business expenses to provide the big picture of its financial performance over several years.

Customer Relationship Management (CRM) Software

As your doula business grows, you may find it difficult to stay organized. Keeping track of intake forms, customer files, signed contracts, etc. is time consuming when done on a larger scale. Customer Relationship Management (CRM) software can help you manage client inquiries, create to-do lists for you and your team, keep track of client contracts and documents, organize business files, and more.

Some of the more popular CRM software for doula businesses include:

- Dubsado
- Basecamp
- 17 Hats

Investing in a good CRM software will allow your business to keep growing, while making it easier for you to manage all of its day-to-day business needs.

Marketing Your Doula Business

Once you have established your doula business, created a website, and organized all of the contracts and forms you will need, then it's time to find clients! In order for clients to find you, you have to market yourself. Marketing strategies can be divided between online - social media, blogging, email marketing campaigns, etc. - and in-person - meeting with providers, hosting events, warm chatting, etc.

Marketing Tips

If It's Free, It's for Me!

- Utilize all of your free options first. Many of the most popular social networking platforms offer free business accounts. It is the most cost effective way to market and advertise a business.
- Network, Network, Network! Schedule your long overdue gynecologist appointment and let your doctor/midwife know of your new venture.
- Be sure to bring professional marketing materials with you and leave a great impression with the office staff. They are the ones who answer the phone when patients call for a doula referral!
- Join a committee that serves the birth world.

- A hospital maternity fair is a great start!
- Contribute to existing birth or postpartum related blogs.

Low Cost Marketing

- Become a Childbirth Educator! Pregnant individuals may not be seeking the supportive services of a doula simply because they don't know what one is. But they do know what childbirth classes are! By becoming a childbirth educator through ProDoula, you will be seen as an expert and will have the opportunity to teach others about all of their birth options, including YOU as their doula!
- Marketing materials. Business cards and rack cards can be printed inexpensively through Vistaprint.
- Offer to bring snacks to another birth professional's childbirth class in exchange for the opportunity to do a short presentation about your services.
- Set up a lunch in a doctor's office to discuss the services that you provide (cost $60 - $100).
- Purchase a table at a birth related fair or show ($50 - $2,000).

Mid-High Range Budget

- Hire a professional web designer to build your website ($2,000 - $15,000).
- Hire a professional to shoot video or "commercials" to post on social media in order to drive traffic to your website ($500 - $5,000).
- Have your car wrapped with your company logo and design ($1,800 – $2,500).
- Rent or lease office space in a high visibility area ($300 - $3000 per month).

Consider participating in programs such as Carrot, state funded doula programs, or setting up your business to accept health saving or flexible spending accounts that allow potential clients to use these forms of insurance to partially or fully cover the expense of doula care. By doing so, you are creating the opportunity to market yourself in an additional way.

Streams of Income for Your Doula Business

The most obvious way to generate income as a doula is of course by providing doula services. As a labor doula or a postpartum doula, you will charge a flat rate or an hourly rate and you will be paid in direct proportion to how often you work. However, your earning potential is not limited to the number of hours you are available.

Consider these other options and allow yourself to explore others as your business grows.

Teach Childbirth Education and Newborn Care Classes

Position yourself as the expert on all things related to childbirth. As more clients enroll in your classes, more and more of them will also hire you to be their doula. Look into ProDoula's childbirth education curriculum and online certification.

Provide Placenta Services

Learning to provide placenta encapsulation services or hiring someone to do it can be financially rewarding and a valuable service for your clientele. For obvious reasons, always adhere to the highest standards when offering and providing these services.

Sell or Rent Products

Be sure to get a tax ID number and collect tax when applicable. Speak to your accountant about setting up the structure to accommodate this.

Growing Your Doula Business

As time goes on and as you take advantage of all the resources ProDoula has for you, your doula business will grow. Regardless of what business model is working for you, you might find yourself in the position to contract with other doulas to provide services.

As you develop name/brand recognition for your doula business more and more potential clients will be contacting you. You will be delighted to see the "fruit of your labor." However, by working independently, you will, at some point, reach the maximum number of clients appropriate to contract with for a given time period, and you will have to turn clients away or refer them to another doula.

Having worked hard to get your name out into the community it will be disappointing to refuse potential clients. Consider hiring other doulas as sub-contractors to work for you. In this scenario, a client hires your business and your business sets a standard of care that is modeled in your "team."

Pay your doulas a flat rate or an hourly rate and retain a portion of the fee for your efforts to acquire the clients, handle the scheduling of shifts, billing, and payroll. The ProDoula team is happy to offer you guidance if this is a direction you would like to grow in.

Goal Setting

When done properly, goal setting can be a very powerful tool. Unfortunately, without being taught how to set goals properly, many of us end up setting half-hearted goals and then feel terrible when we do not reach them.

Although goal setting has obvious value, we bring to each set of goals our feelings and thoughts about the last goal we set. If we succeeded at achieving our last goal, then we are filled with confidence as we tackle our next one. But if we failed at the previous goal or if we perceived it as a failure or feel that we have fallen short, then we will bring those feelings along with us as we begin working on the next goal.

CLEAR THE SLATE! Try it a different way. They say that if you always do what you always did, you'll always get what you always got. If we want something different, we must DO something different!

So, set a goal.

- Ask yourself, "WHAT do I want to accomplish?"
- And then ask yourself, "HOW will I accomplish it?

What is your strategy? You can't start with an "I'll figure it out" model. It must be deliberate. It might work for a short period, but success relies on a well thought out approach to "how."

You must believe you can do it. However, you may need some guidance and support and ProDoula is here to provide it!

Notes: